the UNCYCLOPEDIA of ROCK

the UNCYCLOPEDIA of ROCK

ANGUS DEAYTON
JEREMY PASCALL
GEOFFREY PERKINS

EBURY PRESS
LONDON

Published by Ebury Press
Division of The National Magazine Company Ltd
Colquhoun House
27-37 Broadwick Street
London W1V 1FR

First impression 1987

ISBN 0 85223 612 3

Designed by Millions Design

Computerset by Stratatype Ltd, London
Printed and bound in Great Britain by Butler
& Tanner Ltd, Frome, Somerset

ERRATA
In the bibliography the title of Brian Epstein's book should read 'A Cellarful of Noise' and not 'A Cellarful of Boys' and 'Hip Hop' by Dr. Rodney Trower ND, should be 'Hip Op. – The History of Artificial Hip Replacement Surgery.'
   We apologise for these mistakes.
   We would also like to apologise to The People of Belgium. We are very sorry, it must be awful living there.

CONTENTS

IT SHOOK THE WORLD.

IT CHANGED THE LIVES OF MILLIONS.

IT TOOK THE WEST BY STORM.

IT ALTERED THE COURSE OF HISTORY.

IT WAS THE RUSSIAN REVOLUTION AND QUITE IRRELEVANT TO THE STORY OF ROCK & ROLL.

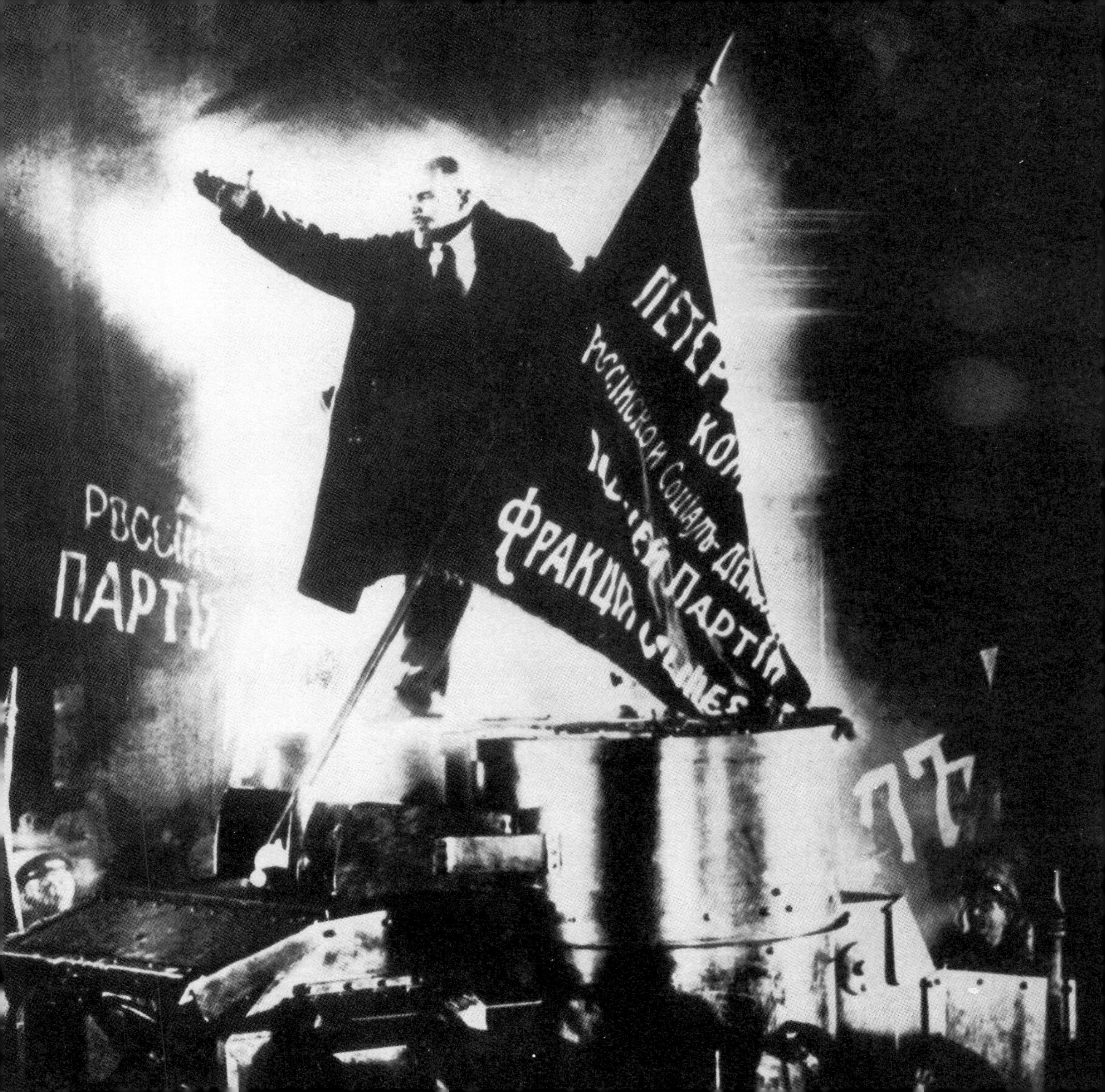

CHAPTER 1

FROM RHYTHM TO BLUES AND BACK

The roots of rock & roll stretch back to eighteenth century Africa and the songs of tribesmen who were captured in the hundreds of thousands for the slave trade. The vast majority of these slaves were exported to the United States which explains why rock & roll was eventually born in America, rather than in, say, Belgium. Although slaves were sold in Belgium, most of them escaped and fled to the Southern States of the U.S., preferring a life of incredible hardship and cruelty in the plantations to the stultifying boredom of living in Brussels.

It was this life of unremitting toil that prompted negroes to develop a heart-rening plaint, bewailing life's cares, that they called 'The Blues', and others were to call 'That Bloody Awful Noise'. Nobody quite knows why these distinctive twelve-bar songs were called 'The Blues' but after intensive research the eminent entomologist, Professor Krimmel of the Department of Linguistics at the University of Peru, Indiana, has posited that they were named after the colour of the underside of a specie of cockroach found only in remote parts of rural Georgia.[1]

Whatever the reason for their name, 'The Blues' were mournful folk songs that invariably started with the words: *I woke up this morning* . . . And then went on to give a minute-by-minute account of the day's catalogue of woe. The songs were, if anything, even more depressing than the life led by the singers.

None of the earliest Blues are still extant, so we don't know exactly what they were like, but contemporary descriptions

Natalie 'Blind Girl' Cohen.

by those unfortunate enough to hear them, indicate they must have been similar to listening non-stop to the entire works of Leonard Cohen, but not quite as cheerful.

Rural blues were also known as 'field songs', because they had to be sung miles away from human habitation after neighbours, complaining about the dreadful noise, had driven the singers away by throwing rocks at them. Some authorities claim this to be the derivation of the term 'rock music', while others insist it is the first, but far from the last, report of musicians being stoned. Both theories can be treated with contempt.

The rural blues developed very little for a hundred years, except that they got longer and drearier. Some were so long that they started with the line: *I woke up one morning, a month ago last Thursday* . . .[2] They were usually sung 'a capella' – mean-

ing while wearing a cap – and it wasn't until early in the century that they changed significantly.

THE FIRST BREAKTHROUGH WAS ...

The first breakthrough was when a Mississippi blues-shouter – Nat 'Blind Boy' Cohen – was introduced to a guitar. The effect on 'Blind Boy' was immediate and sensational, no sooner had he felt the guitar in his hands than he fell in love with it, proposed and eloped to Chicago.

It was on the honeymoon night, while attempting to make love to the guitar – predating Jimi Hendrix and Prince by fifty years – that he discovered two things. First, that the guitar made interesting noises. And second, that men attempting to mate with guitars made interesting noises, especially when sensitive parts of their anatomies came into violent contact with the strings. Thus on that one night, 'Blind Boy' pioneered the guitar solo and the characteristic shout or holler, 'Aaaaaaayeeeee!', which was to punctuate rock songs over the years.

When 'Blind Boy' was finally released

[1] Other experts have dismissed this theory, calling it 'specious', 'logically erroneous' and 'complete bollocks'. And have challenged the wisdom of appointing an entomologist, rather than an etymologist, to a linguistics department. As Professor Krimmel has subsequently transferred to the Department of Aberrant Psychology at the University of Peru, Indiana, as an in-patient, the theory may be safely ignored. Not least because the Georgia in question is a Soviet state of Russia where very few, if any, negro slaves were ever kept and therefore has no relevance to the story of rock although, interestingly, it does have some relevance to the Russian Revolution. See *The Seminal Role Of The Cockroach In The Russian Revolution* by the same authors.

[2] A report that this particular blues song, which was started in 1874, remains unfinished and is currently being sung by the great-great-great grandson of the original composer, remains unconfirmed as no one has had the guts to investigate.

from hospital, he started playing his guitar in Chicago clubs and found considerable local fame as Natalie 'Blind Girl' Cohen, the first sex-change blues singer.

The guitar brought a new urgency to the traditional blues. In short it brought rhythm. This became known as 'Rhythm and blues'. Or, simply, 'R&B', to distinguish it from 'B&B' which was developing at the same time in Britain. However, Bed and Breakfast plays little part in the story of rock.

THE WAR YEARS

The war years, 1939-1945 (for most countries except America, which was too busy between '39 and '41 to take part), had very little effect on Rhythm and Blues and none whatsoever on rock & roll, which still hadn't been invented. However, after the war things were to change swiftly. And the reason for the change was radio.

AFTER THE WAR

In the early 1950s America was still a country divided by race. The blacks and whites were segregated. Blacks had their own music, their own records and their own radio stations. This was patently unfair and unjust, particularly to young whites who were forced to listen to 'crooners', ageing men in toupees, who had all the rhythm, soul and sex appeal of boiled cabbage. Mainstream white radio played nothing else. Desperate for something more exciting the young started to twiddle their knobs. And then they started to twiddle their radio dials. What they found were black stations pumping out black music and the seeds of rock & roll were sown.

Jimi Hendrix in one of his early beach movies.

CHAPTER 2

FROM ROLL TO ROCK & VICE VERSA

The day is Tuesday, February 21st. The year is 1952. The place is Cleveland, Ohio. The weather is changeable, occasionally sunny with scattered showers, and a low of 2°C (34°F), so wrap up warm.

On this day, in this year, in this city, in this weather, a man called Allen Freed is about to change history. Another man called Alan Freed is about to change his shirt. It is this Alan Freed, in his clean, warmer shirt, who concerns us. The other Freed, no relation, would have played an important part had he not suffered a fatal heart attack just as he was about to change history and was thus relegated to a mere footnote in the story of rock & roll.[3]

Alan Freed was a disc jockey working for an unpopular, middle-of-the-road radio station. The reason it was unpopular was

[3] Allen Freed

Allen Freed wearing his first hearing aid.

because it was situated in the middle of Roosevelt Road, causing vast traffic jams.

Freed had other reasons to be depressed, he was thirty years old, unsuccessful, pock-marked and deaf in one ear. However, on this day, as he was walking to work, he was suddenly stopped short by a sound coming from a record store. Freed had never heard music like it. In fact, Freed had never really heard music at all, owing to his deafness.

Fascinated, Freed walked into the store and talked to the owner, Leo Glintz, who remembers that day well:–

66 This guy walks in off the street and says: 'What's this music? So I tells him.

And if I live to be a hundred I'll never forget what he said to me. Alan Freed looks at me and he says: 'Pardon?'

So I tells him again and he says 'Pardon?' again. So I write it down on a piece of paper and he says, 'I gotta have these records.' So I sell him a whole stack of them. And the next thing I know he's playing them on his show.

Alan Freed, was the first white DJ to play this kinda music on the radio and I put it down to the fact that the poor guy was deaf as a doorpost. 99

Alan Freed went on air with a show he called *Moondog's Rock & Roll Party*. Freed was probably not the first person to coin the phrase 'rock & roll', but he certainly introduced it into common parlance. What does 'rock & roll' actually mean? Again the experts are divided.

Charlie Ronson, the Rock Correspondent of *The National Geographic Magazine* and Visiting Professor of Comparative

Creativity at the University of Life, Southern California. In an interview with the authors he said:

66 The term 'rock & roll' has a deeply sexual connotation, something that must be evident even to mental pigmies like yourselves. It is, in fact, a euphemism for the act of fornication. When you hear Bill Haley exhorting you to 'rock around the clock', he's not suggesting you take part in some dance marathon, what he's actually encouraging you to do, is bonk yourself brainless 24 hours a day.

Interestingly, the song itself only lasted two-and-a-half minutes which, apparently was the average time Bill Haley could manage. He was, after all, a very old and extremely fat person. 99

So, are we to assume that 'rock & roll' is a euphemism for sex? Not according to Doctor Fitzgerald, Professor of Lyricology at St. Geldof's, Oxford:

66 It's time someone scotched this ludicrous theory. Look at it logically: when I go to a cafeteria and order a rock cake, am I asking for a rock cake or a 'sex cake'? The answer is obvious. When I order a ham roll, I'm not asking for a 'ham sex', am I? And, of course, when I go to the coast and pick up a rock on the beach, I'm not picking up sex,

rock & roll fame, as Charlie Ronson observes:—

66 *Bill Haley was thirty years old, short and balding. He didn't look like a rock & roller, but as soon as he got on stage and started singing 'Rock Around The Clock', he really got the girls screaming.*

Not surprising, really. God, he was ugly. He scared the pants off those girls. And let's face it, the poor guy couldn't get the pants off them any other way. 99

So, what was the secret of his success? Veteran manager, agent and entrepreneur, Sam Chuck, describes himself as 'The Friend To All The Stars' and claims to have put dozens of rock stars on the road to success:—

66 *I remember I was sitting in my office one day in 1955 when Bill Haley came in. He said to me, 'Mr. Chuck,' he said, 'I'm thirty years old, short and balding and I want to be a rock & roll star.' And I said to him, 'Brush your hair into a ridiculous kiss curl, record a song called "Crazy Man Crazy" and you'll be a big star.' And he said, 'Thanks, Mr. Chuck, I'll do that' and that's what he did and that's how he became a star.* 99

'Crazy, Man, Crazy' was the first rock & roll song to make the American charts. But the song that really introduced rock & roll to a wide public was 'Rock Around The Clock' with its haunting and lyrical reflections on the transient nature of time:—

66 *One o'clock, two o'clock, three o'clock, rock!* 99

---

am I? Well, as it, happens, I am. But I hardly think that's relevant to an analysis of rock & roll. 99

Despite Doctor Fitzgerald's disclaimer, there's no denying that rock & roll was very sexy music which appealed instantly to young people, making Freed's show the most popular in Cleveland. Soon his popularity was noted in New York and he was

Above Bill Haley modelling his early Phil Collins look.

signed by station W.I.M.P. where he became known as 'The Father of Rock & Roll'.

Soon Freed was to introduce the first rock & roll star, Bill Haley, who was to become known as 'The Uncle of Rock & Roll'. He was an unlikely candidate for

The classic opening line of 'Rock Around The Clock' set kids dancing across the world. The man responsible for its success was Mort Stein:–

66 *Bill Haley's manager called me in and told me Bill needed my help. And so Haley and I locked ourselves away in a hotel room for three days. We worked day and night, just stopping for the occasional sandwich and sex, but it was worth it. After seventy-two tough, exhausting hours, Bill had mastered counting all the way up to twelve. Admittedly, he didn't always get the numbers in the right order, sometimes he would sing: 'One o'clock, two o'clock, five o'clock, rock', but most people didn't notice. And, of course, the kids didn't care, all they were interested in was the beat. And bonking themselves brainless.* 99

'Rock Around The Clock' became a major hit when it was featured in the motion picture, *Blackboard Jungle*.[4] And shortly after Bill Haley became the star of the first rock movie called, with typical Hollywood originality, *Rock Around The Clock*. The producer was Walt Dientz:–

66 *That movie was lensed on a very small budget, but went on to make millions. You know, when I think of* Rock Around The Clock, *I think of big bucks. Big bucks, enormous antelopes and giant elks – these were some of the creatures we were going to feature in the movie, we wanted to have them threaten New York City while Bill Haley was playing* the Rockefeller Center.

In fact, Haley was going to play the hero who saved New York City from destruction but unfortunately he wasn't much of an actor. So instead, we got him to play a fat, ageing, bald rock & roll star with a kiss curl. And we also got him to play 'Rock Around The Clock' sixteen times in the film. He didn't play either very well, but the kids didn't seem to mind. 99

'The kids' loved the movie and they showed their approval by shouting, screaming, dancing in the aisles and smashing up the cinemas, Randy Schwartz, now a forty-nine-year old accountant with two children and a heart by-pass operation, was sixteen in 1955 and remembers going to his local movie house in Dayton, Ohio:–

66 *Yeah, we were crazy in those days! A gang of us kids went alaong to the Roxy and we just went mad! We started by slashing the seat covers with our flick knives, then we pulled the seats out of the floor and flung them at the screen. Next someone had the idea of going up into the projection room and smashing the equipment! Just as we were about to do that, we were stopped by the theater manager. So we hurled him through the window and out onto the street! Just a load of kids fooling around!*

Only trouble was, I never actually got to see the movie, but I'll never forget the sight of that manager hitting the sidewalk! Yeah, those were the days, we had to make our own fun then, didn't have TV or nothing. 99

The huge success of *Rock Around The Clock* persuaded Hollywood to make a fol-low-up movie, *Don't Knock the Rock*, this was followed in turn by *Don't Knock The Clock*, *Don't Clock The Knock* and finally, as inspiration waned, *Rock Clock Don't The*.

The Establishment reacted with horror at the effects of rock & roll. Dr. Fitzgerald:–

66 *At first the authorities tried to ignore rock & roll, then to ban and even legislate against it. Rock & rollers were shunned, mocked, despised, abused and harassed by the police. Some were even subjected to the greatest humiliation of all – their pocket money was stopped and they were sent to bed without any supper.* 99

But despite these draconian measures, rock & roll was, in the words of the song, here to stay.

Danny & The Juniors' hit, 'Rock & Roll Is Here To Stay' was one of the more comprehensible songs of the period. One of the least intelligible was by Little 'The Nephew Of Rock & Roll' Richard: Tutti Frutti oh Rooty.

Do these words mean anything? The eminent lyricologist, Dr. Fitzgerald:–

---

[4]This was the story of an idealistic young teacher who is posted to a tough school and tries to win the trust of a class of juvenile delinquents by playing them his treasured collection of jazz records. They respond to his caring attention by stomping his discs to pieces. This violent scene was greeted by a public outcry and demands for something to be done. The record industry responded swiftly, very soon it introduced the vinyl disc, which was more difficult to smash than the 78 and, ultimately, the virtually indestructible Compact Disc.

Right *Little Richard, so called because he had a very small richard.*

ὦ *The title – 'Tutti Frutti' – refers to a type of Italian ice cream, a multi-flavoured variety that we British know as 'Neapolitan'. 'Oh rooti' is, I suggest, a corruption of the French phrase 'en route', meaning on the way. Thus 'Tutti-frutti en route' means that the Italian ice cream is on the way.*

As for 'AWOPBOBALOOBOPALOP-BAMBOOM', Let's break it down into its constituent parts.

'A wop bop', is quite evidently an Italian dance, reinforcing the Italianate theme of the whole work. 'A loo bop' means they're obviously dancing in the toilet. So, to summarise, we have some Italians dancing in a lavatory.

And, finally, we come to 'Alopbamboom'. This, I think, admits of a a simple explanation: it's complete gibberish, I think Little Richard must have been out of his mind.

And I think this is why Little Richard was an international success. Songs like 'Tutti Frutti' meant exactly the same in New York, Paris, Berlin and Tokyo – absolutely nothing. ὧ

However, rock & roll wasn't to find international success until the music had created a star, someone younger, sexier and thinner than Bill Haley and less obviously unhinged than Little Richard. A man destined to be the first superstar of rock and who would go on to even greater fame by giving his name to a man with spectacles called Costello.

Right *Elvis Presley?*
(Please check before
going to print).

CHAPTER 3

ELVIS PRESLEY

Elvis Aaron Presley was destined for fame. he was destined to become famous as Tennessee's greatest Brussel sprouts grower but fate pitched him into another career, that of the undisputed King of Rock & Roll.

When asked, towards the end of his life, whether he'd have been happier growing Brussel sprouts than as a huge megastar, surrounded by wealth, fame and women, he said:–

"*Oggly boggly diddle mumph cheese- burger.***"**

A tragic indictment of the toll drugs had taken on him. One of his aides translated his ramblings as:–

"*No.***"**

Very shortly after his birth, his parents, Gladys and Vernon, moved from Tupelo, Mississippi, to Memphis, Tennessee, but somehow the infant Elvis found out where they were and crawled all the way to join them. As he later said, his mother was an enormous influence on him. He claimed he had named his sumptuous mansion in her memory, but as it was called 'Grace- land' rather than 'Gladysland', this must also be put down to drugs.

It is generally thought that Presley's drug abuse started in his later years, but one of his aides, Red Hopkirk, tells a dif- ferent story:–

Right *Elvis Presley before his hole-in-the- hand operation.*

"*Elvis was into drug abuse in his twenties. I often used to go into his bathroom and find him standing in front of the medicine chest, swearing at packets of aspirins, and screaming insults at bottles of cough linctus. He thought they were talking about him behind his back. He was incredibly paranoid, I guess it was all the cocaine he was taking.***"**

There has been much dispute about Presley's drug habit. One man who claims to know the truth is Carl Schreibner M.D., who was Presley's doctor for the last two years of his life:–

"*Some people say Elvis was a hopeless drug addict. Others disagree and say he was a very enthusias- tic drug addict. I dis- agree with both.*** **Elvis wasn't an addict at all. He just enjoyed taking incredible amounts of drugs.***"**

But back in the early 1940s, in Memphis, Elvis was just an ordinary little boy who showed exceptional musical ability at an early age on both piano and guitar. He'd play along to songs on the radio by beating the piano with the guitar.

Elvis grew up listening to black music as well as the Country & Western records played by white stations like K.K.K., run by the Ku Klux Klan. He was influenced by both, developing his own hybrid style which he played to anyone who would listen. And when he ran out of people who would listen he played and sang to himself, which is when Sam 'Friend To All The Stars' Chuck first met him and claims to have put him on the road to stardom:–

66 *I met Elvis Presley one day, he was just sitting in the corner of a barn, strumming his guitar and I said, 'Hey, son, brush your hair back, wiggle your hips, record a song called "That's Alright, Mama" and you'll be The King of Rock & Roll.' And he said, 'Thank you very much, Mr. Chuck, I'll do that.' And that's how he started.* 99

Another man who put Elvis on the road to stardom was Sam Phillips – the man who was to become known as The Godfather of Rock & Roll – owner of the small Sun recording studio in Memphis. Working there was a man who was to become known as The Step-Father of Rock & Roll, engineer Frank Delano:–

66 *Sam Phillips was a man with a vision, he could see a new sound in his mind's ear and he was obsessed with finding this sound. He thought it would be a fusion of rhythm and blues and country music. He was looking for a white guy who could sing like a black guy and*

after months of searching, Sam finally heard about this white boy who had everything – good looks, sexy movements and best of all he sang like a negro.

He'd been playing odd gigs around Memphis and Sam set about tracking him down. He finally found him hanging around a bar. Not so much hanging around it, as hanging in it, from a beam. The Ku Klux

Klan got him. In them days, the Klan didn't like white boys who sang like negroes. 99

Phillips returned to Sun a disappointed man but in the meantime the studio had been visited by Elvis Presley who had

Below *The wild world of Rock & Roll took its toll – Frankie Lyman at the age of 21.*

come in to make a record as a present for his mother's birthday. The studio receptionist was Marlene Frick – known as The Half-Sister Of Rock & Roll – who was immediately impressed by the young Presley:–

66 *There was something about him. No, it wasn't his voice, nor his guitar playing. It was something else, something I couldn't put my finger on. I tried to but he wouldn't let me. In those days he was a very shy kid and didn't like people touching his pelvis.* 99

Marlene told Sam Phillips about Elvis and within days Presley was back in the Sun studios recording a blues song called 'That's Alright, Mama'. With Presley's first record, Phillips had finally achieved a fusion between black and white music; the result was a sort of sludgey grey music. Nonetheless, Phillips thought it was the greatest thing since sliced bread. But nobody else agreed with him, mainly because sliced bread wouldn't be invented for another two years.

However, some people did agree that Phillips had made a musical breakthrough, but success didn't come easily. Phillips managed to get 'That's Alright, Mama' played on stations all round the South but that didn't help as a lot people hated listening to rock & roll while they were waiting for a train. Then he tried bus stations but that was no better. In desperation, he took the record to a few radio stations and things finally started happening.

Right *Elvis Presley and the Midgets.*

Before long Presley was playing live gigs and the crowd reaction was incredible. As early as 1954 Elvis caused a riot in Jacksonville, Florida. Incredible because at the time he was appearing in Osmondville, Kentucky.

Despite such enthusiasm, Elvis was still only big in the south – and, indeed, below the Mason-Dixon line. He needed an astute business manager who could market him to the major recording companies in New York.

At this point the man who was to become known as The Second Cousin Twice Removed of Rock & Roll, Colonel Tom Parker, enters the story. Parker's only previous business experience was running a fast food restaurant selling deep fried fountain pens but nevertheless he got Elvis signed to R.C.A. and in 1955 the label released 'Heartbreak Hotel' which went to number one all around the world and within a year Presley had became the first rock megastar.

Suddenly, the poor boy from Memphis found himself one of the most famous people in the world. What effect did this have on a gauche 20-year-old from the sticks? His childhood friend, Orville Felt:

66 *Well, suddenly Elvis was fabulously wealthy and incredibly famous. Women threw themselves at him. And if they didn't he had two guys who would pick them up and throw them.* 99

In 1956 Elvis made his first movie, *Love Me Tender* and yet again, teen reaction was astonishing. As soon as Elvis came up on the screen, larger than life, the kids couldn't control themselves, they just burst into tears; mostly because he was such a lousy actor. But in fairness, he did have screen presence and occasionally he resembled the great Thirties movie stars – the same facial expression, the same way of moving and delivering his lines. Yes, occasionally, Elvis was tremendously reminiscent of Rin Tin Tin.

Despite this, Elvis had a long movie career. The man who produced just under half of his films – 370 of them – was Sol Herzog:–

66 *Working on Elvis's movies was quite an experience and what with getting all the songs and scripts written, plus the actual shooting, editing, post-production and so on, well, a film could take anything up to a day-and-a-half to make. Maybe two full days if Elvis had to walk and talk at the same time.* 99

Curiously, this remorseless grind of filming had very little adverse affect on Elvis's career. In fact, nothing seemed to affect his popularity, not even two years in the army. Presley was drafted on 24th March, 1958. One of his buddies at training camp was Don Stewart:–

66 *Elvis was just a regular guy, you know, I never saw him play the big temperamental star. Except when the Commanding Officer told him he was being posted to Germany. Elvis really blew his top and refused to be posted there. No, he demanded to be sent on a plane like everyone else, Elvis was a nice guy, but he had the I.Q. of a cabbage.* 99

Some authorities maintain that Presley's army service in Germany had a lasting and detrimental affect on him. Certainly, on his return to America, he was no longer the raunchy rocker he'd once been. From producing great records like 'Blue Suede Shoes', 'Hound Dog' and 'All Shook UP', he now churned out schmaltzy ballads like 'It's Now Or Never' and 'Wooden Heart', an old Bavarian folk song which told of a young Tyrolean boy's unrequited love for a beautiful but faithless goat.

Some believe the change was due to Presley's increasing maturity, others because he had fallen in love with a sixteen-year-old girl called Priscilla Beaulieu, others because he'd fallen in love with a beautiful but faithless goat and still others, like the historian, Professor Eugene Flint, have an alternative theory:–

66 *In my opinion, the Elvis Presley who returned from Germany was not the same man who went into the army. He was a completely different man called Fritz Gemuchtlicht, an East German look-alike who was substituted by the Commies for the real Presley, who they held in Spandau Jail and passed off as Rudolph Hess.*[5] 99

Whatever the truth, Presley was still The King, but he had forsaken rock & roll which, back in 1956, was developing stars who stood in the young Elvis's shadow. But not so much in his shadow as they did 20 years later when he was so fat that when he arrived in Las Vegas he caused a total eclipse of the sun.

[5]Professor Flint is now sharing a room with Professor Krimmel at the Department of Aberrant Psychology at the University of Peru, Indiana.

CHAPTER 4

OTHER QUITE FAMOUS PEOPLE WHO ALSO PLAYED ROCK & ROLL

Although Elvis Presley was undoubtedly The King, there were many pretenders to his throne. Foremost Buddy Holly – the man who became known as The Prince of Rock & Roll. Charles Hardin Holly was born in Lubbock, Texas, but despite that misfortune, he made an early start in music as a Country singer, singing songs about Patagonia, Bechuana and even Belgium.

Soon he turned to rock & roll but his early records were flops, so he contacted Sam 'Friend to All the Stars' Chuck:–

I remember the day Buddy Holly came to my office. He said, 'Mr. Chuck, I wanna be a rock & roll star.' And I told him, 'The first thing you should do, Buddy, is get yourself a pair of horn-rimmed glasses.' And he said, 'Will that turn me into a star?' And I said, 'Maybe not, but it'll stop you talking to hat-stands.' And he said, 'Thanks Mr. Chuck, that's what I'll do.' And he turned round and walked straight into the door and he says, 'Whoops-a-daisy!' And I say to him, 'You should write a song with that line in it.' And he said, 'That'll be the day.' And I said, 'No, call it "It Doesn't Matter Any More".' And that's what he did and that's how he became a star.

Holly's rise to fame was rapid but cut tragically short by a plane crash that also

Above It takes more than a fatal plane crash to keep these early rockers down!

claimed the lives of Ritchie Valens and The Big Bopper. Fate, however, took a hand with someone else who was supposed to have been with them:–

Yeah, I was supposed to have been on that flight but then, at the last moment, I just didn't make it.

Call it second sight, or something, but somehow I feel that had I gone, the crash wouldn't have happened. You see, I was the pilot.

Buddy Holly, undoubtedly one of the most talented musicians of his day, was only twenty-two when he was killed, who knows what he'd have gone on to achieve, if he'd lived? Charlie Ronson:–

❝Holly would be in his fifties now and I believe he'd have gone on to enjoy a long, successful and distinguished career. I think he'd probably be the vice-president of one of the major banks. He was uniquely qualified for the job – those horn-rimmed glasses, that puny little body, let's face it, he looked like a banker. Yes, if he'd been alive today, he'd be in his 25th year in banking and as miserable as sin.

Just as well he died when he did. ❞

THE ARCHDUKE OF R&R

A man even more suited to the role of bank manager was Chuck Berry – The Arch-duke of Rock & Roll – who was legendary not only for his music, but also for his meanness. Ronnie Kent who frequently played on the same bill as Berry while backing Buddy Holly remembers:–

❝Chuck Berry has this rule that he wouldn't go on stage until he was paid. Well, one night he'd played his set and the crowd loved it and started hollering for encores, but Berry wouldn't go back on until he'd been paid extra. The promoter was pretty pissed-off at this and to get his own back he gave Chuck the money in nickels and dimes. Chuck shoved them in his jacket pockets and ran back on stage, but he was so weighed down by the coins that he could only move with a stoop. And that's how Chuck Berry's famous 'duck walk' was invented. ❞

Despite his tight-fistedness, no one disputes that Chuck Berry wrote some of the greatest rock & roll songs of all time. Dr. Fitzgerald:–

❝ *Perhaps Berry's finest song was 'Rock & Roll Music' which has been described as the first rock & roll anthem. This is not strictly true, Berry wrote a tune before that which was, by any standards, an anthem. In fact, it was 'The Stars And Stripes Forever' and it's a measure of Berry's genius that, no sooner had he written it than he thought it sounded familiar, tore it up and started again.* ❞

'Rock & Roll Music' inspired other musicians like Carl 'The Duke of Rock & Roll' Perkins, Pat 'The Earl of Rock & Roll' Boone and the legendary Little Richard, the man who was to be the biggest influence on Eighties star, Prince (known as the Commoner of Rock & Roll).

OTHER NOT-QUITE-SO FAMOUS PEOPLE WHO ALSO PLAYED ROCK & ROLL

The man known as The Baron of Rock & Roll, but who called himself 'The Killer', was Jerry Lee Lewis. His stage act was outrageous and, to other musicians, notorious. Buddy Holly's backing musician, Ronnie Kent:–

❝ *I remember Jerry Lee would start hammering the piano with his fists, then he'd kick the piano stool across the stage. Next he'd pick up the mike stand and hurl it at the drums. Then he'd fetch an axe and start chopping up the stage and then he'd take a can of kerosene and set fire to it. Yep, he was a hard act to follow. Mostly because there weren't no stage left to play on once he'd finished.* ❞

Remarkably, it wasn't these antics that nearly destroyed Lewis, but the scandal

Below *Jerry Lee Lewis*

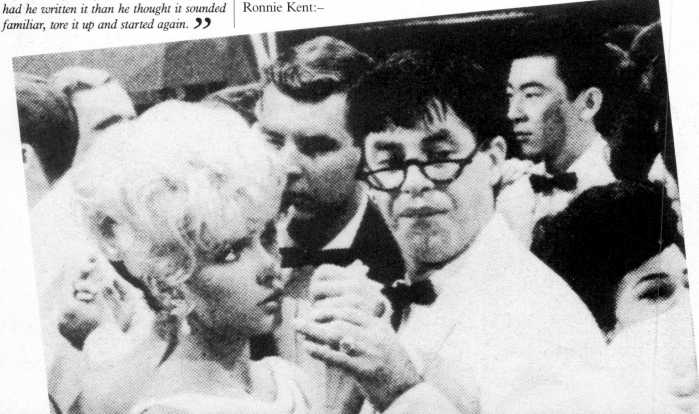

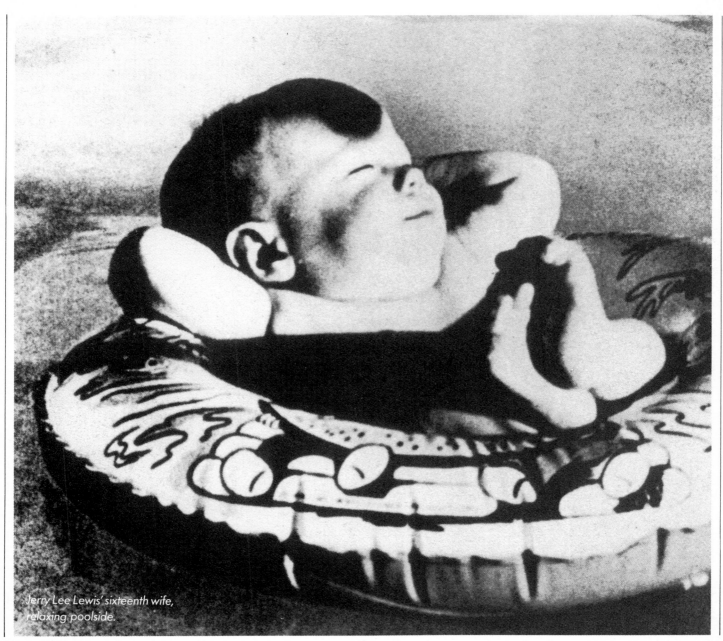

Jerry Lee Lewis' sixteenth wife, relaxing poolside.

25

surrounding his marriage to a thirteen-year-old girl. Predictably the marriage didn't last, after a few months he divorced her on the grounds of incompatibility because she refused to tie her own shoe laces, and he ran off with an older woman, her fifteen-year-old babysitter. Other marriages followed but it wasn't until the Eighties that Jerry Lee Lewis announced he'd settled down for good with a girl who was old enough to be his great-granddaughter.

The furore about Jerry Lee Lewis's first marriage broke while he was on tour in Britain and, ironically, it was in Britain where Eddie Cochran met his death in a car crash in 1960. On the strength of his two classic singles – 'Summertime Blues' and 'C'mon Everybody' – Cochran seemed set to challenge Presley's domination. Charlie Ronson:–

❝ *In my opinion, which, in my opinion, is the correct opinion, had Cochran lived, he could have been like Elvis. Probably impotent and incontinent, alcoholic and a drug addict. In fact, very similar to Presley before his death, a shambling wreck with the I.Q. of a boiled egg. He'd be stumbling around the stage of a Las Vegas casino, bursting out of a pair of flared trousers, weighed down by massive gold medallions and mouthing garbage like 'My Way'.* **❞**

Travelling in the same car as Cochran was Gene Vincent – 'The Secretary of the Interior of Rock & Roll' – who miraculously

Gene Vincent being helped on stage by Hurricane Higgins, four hours after his death.

survived the crash and whose career was tragically to last another eleven years.

Vincent was mean, moody, magnificent and another word beginning with 'm' culled from *Roget's Thesaurus*. His threatening, bad boy image was carefully modelled on his movie star heroes.

He took his vulnerable, hunched posture from James Dean in *Rebel Without A Cause*... He borrowed the black leather motor-bike gear from Marlon Brando in *The Wild One*... The greasy slicked-back hair and glowering look came from Elvis Presley in *King Creole*... And the painful limping walk came from watching Kenneth More in *Reach For The Sky*...

Despite these potent stars, by the end of the Fifties, the power of rock & roll was waning. Elvis Presley was in the army, Jerry Lee Lewis was in disgrace, Chuck Berry was in the counting-house counting out his money and Little Richard was in the throes of religious ecstacy having found God, although until he declared this to the world, nobody had realised that He was missing.

More devastating still, Ritchie Valens, The Big Bopper, Eddie Cochran and Buddy Holly were all dead, an appalling toll considering that rock was still in its infancy and, according to Charlie Ronson, a sinister omen of what was to come:–

Above Kenneth More, the Bader boy of rock.

❝ *In my opinion, which, of course, is the correct opinion, there's more to these tragedies than meets the eye. One factor connects these deaths. And that is: sales. Do you realise that after Buddy Holly's death, he sold three times more records than he did when he was alive?* Same goes for Eddie Cochran and the rest.

Now, I'm not saying that the record industry actually arranged these 'accidents' but they were very convenient.

Of course, the real tragedy was Bill Haley. He had the misfortune to die of natural causes. The poor bastard couldn't do anything right. If only he'd had the sense to die younger, he'd be a far wealthier man today. **❞**

CHAPTER 5

1960-1962
THE INTERESTING YEARS

Nineteen-Sixty was a year like any other containing, as it did, 52 weeks, broken down into twelve months. Few people could have prophesied, as the decade changed at midnight on December 31st, 1959, that the Sixties was to be an extraordinary period in the history of pop music. And fewer still could have prophesied that the axis of rock would swing from America to Britain. Only one person prophesied that this year would see the outbreak of The Second World War. He was Auguste Bertrand, a Belgian who thought it was still 1939.

As the new year was rung in, something extraordinary was happening in a back-to-back terrace house in a small street in Liverpool. At that time, on that night, a new sound was heard in 23 Sevastopol Street. It was the sound of a baby crying. And that baby was to change the face of pop music because, only eighteen years later, he was to become Boy George's make-up artist.

Meanwhile, in another part of Liverpool, in a small, steamy cellar, a new sound was heard for the first time. The sound of six washing machines, this was the first launderette to be opened in what would become The Beat Capital of the World. But that was still two years away, in the meantime in Liverpool, as in other British cities, pop music was still dominated by America.[6]

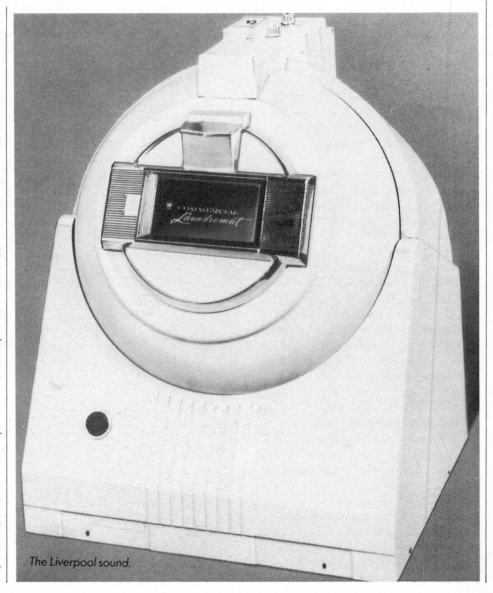

The Liverpool sound.

[6]It's been several pages since the last footnote.

And American music was dominated by singers like Frankie Avalon (né Francis Avallone). He was typical of the new breed of pop stars – Fabian (né Fabiano Bonaparte), Bobby Rydell (né Ridarelli) and, of course, Randy Ney (né Neigh) who dominated the American charts in the early 60s. Most of them came from Philadelphia and they had several other things in common: They were young, they were ambitious, they suffered from acne, but they sang like birds. Frankie Avalon, for example, sang like a vulture, Fabian like a penguin and Bobby Rydell like an ostrich.

There were plenty of young hopefuls in Philadelphia just waiting to be discovered and, as manager Bernie Oberdorff remembers, singing ability was unimportant:–

" *In those days I could literally pick up a good-looking kid off the street and do what I liked with him. But the police put a stop to that. So then I used to hold auditions and if the kid looked right, well, we had coaches to do the rest: there was a singing coach, a dance coach, a speech coach, an autograph coach – who taught them to sign their own names, preferably in joined-up writing – an acting coach and, most important of all, a motor coach, preferably a fast one so that we could get the kid away quickly after the gigs.* **"**

To this day the question remains: were the pop stars of the early Sixties accomplished performers in their own right or were they merely puppets manipulated by powerful managers? We asked several and they all answered unequivocally that we'd have to speak to their managers.

Certainly the pop business of the early

Paul Anka, the well known rhyming slang, who is not mentioned in the text at all.

29

Sixties was run by a handful of highly influential people including Alan 'The Father of Rock & Roll' Freed and Dick 'The Adoptive Son-in-Law of Rock & Roll' Clark, the man who hosted TV's *American Bandstand*.

So powerful were they that it was said Dick Clark could break a star just by refusing to book him on *Bandstand* and that Freed could break a star just by hitting him with a sledgehammer.

The authorities became concerned that these two men could dominate the music industry and investigated claims that they had both received 'payola' from record companies to plug discs and book acts on their shows. Dick Clark was exonerated but Alan Freed admitted that in return for playing certain records he had once been given several dishes of Spanish stew by a record company and was convicted of receiving paella. He never worked again and died shortly after, some said of a broken heart, others said of ptomaine poisoning.

There's no doubt that Dick Clark had enormous influence on the pop world, *American Bandstand* was integral to the creation of such stars as Ricky Nelson, Duane ('The Twang') Eddy – so-called because he put the distinctive 'twanging' sound into the guitar – Eddy ('The Twat') Duane – so-called because he thought nobody would realise he had reversed Duane Eddy's name and because he put the distinctive 'keraking' sound into the guitar by accidentally sitting on it. In addi-

Left *The big 'O' – as enjoyed by many women in the sixties.*

tion Clark promoted the careers of Conway Twitty (né Harold Jenkins), Harold Jenkins (né Dingbat Penis) and perhaps the most successful of them all, Roy Orbison (né Roy Orbison).

Orbison came from the same Memphis stable as Elvis Presley as Sam 'Friend To All The Stars' Chuck remembers:–

❝*I was passing this stable in Memphis and living in it were Roy Orbison and Elvis Presley – they were real poor in them days. I recall it was a real sunny day and Roy Orbison took out a pair of sunglasses, like to protect his eyes from the sun and I said, 'That's it, Roy! Them glasses are your trademark.' And he said, 'Thanks, Mr. Chuck.' And then I said, 'Get yourself known as "The Big O" and go out there and make folks happy.' And that's what he did and that's how he became a star.* ❞

While Orbison was scoring massively in the States, and also making lots of hits, what was happening in The Beat Capital of the World, Liverpool?

LIVERPOOL

In a small back room of a modest house something was about to burst on an unsuspecting world. It was a large pustule on the back of Paul McCartney's neck. It burst as he was listening to the radio which was playing the new music that was sweeping the country. It was called Trad Jazz and it is some measure of the way in which British youth had its finger on the pop pulse that it had been played in New Orleans for over 70 years but it had a remarkable effect on Paul McCartney, he

hated it so much that he decided to move to Hamburg in Germany. A decision that was to prove fateful . . .

Meanwhile, pop music was still dominated by America and by the songsmiths of Tin Pan Alley.

TIN PAN ALLEY

In the early Sixties hardly any pop stars wrote their own songs. Few could read or write music and fewer still could read or write at all. Instead they relied on the work, of professional writers who churned out songs in so-called 'hit factories'. One of these was run by Dan Benton who became known as 'The Man With The Golden Ear' for his unerring ability to recognise a hit tune, copy it, change it slightly, add new words and sell it to a producer like Tony DeSallis who became known as 'The Man With The Tin Ear' for his unerring inability to recognise a plagiarised song.

Benton and his team of writers worked in a suite of offices in New York's Brill Building (which was opposite The Triff Building and just down the street from The Really Amazingly Fab Building). One of the team was Mort 'The Man With The Wooden Leg' Stein:–

❝*I wrote songs for people like Bobby Darin. I never actually wrote for Darin himself but I wrote for people like him. Rock Clinch, for example, was very like Bobby Darin, they could almost be twins. I wrote songs like 'Stupid Cupid' for him. Some were so like 'Stupid Cupid' that we didn't dare release them in America for fear of being sued. One was called 'Not Much Between The Ears'. It was big in Belgium.* ❞

Other writers in The Brill Building, who not only wrote hits for other stars but also for themselves, were Neil Sedaka and Carole King. Sedaka's first big hit was 'Oh! Carole!' written because he was in love with Carole King. She replied with 'Oh! Neil!'. He then wrote another for her called 'Oh! King!' and she riposted with 'Oh! Sedaka.' Then Carole King got married to Gerry Goffin and Sedaka wrote 'Oh! Shit!' which terminated the relationship.

DANCE CRAZES

Although he went on to write many more hits, Sedaka never succeeded in inventing a dance craze. Other writers came up with The Wah-Watusi, The Bristol Stomp, The Mashed Potato, The Hully Gully and, of course, The Wallop...

1 This involved hand-jiving with your partner...
2 Twirling her around in an anti-clockwise direction...
3 Side-stepping twice to the left... And twice to the right...
4 Clapping your hands four times behind your back...
  And twice above your head...
5 Swinging your partner between your legs...
6 And finally having sexual intercourse with her.

Although The Wallop was hugely popular with teens, it never reached the heights of popularity achieved by The Twist, possibly because Twisting was even easier than Walloping and avoided the inevitably hefty dry cleaning bills.

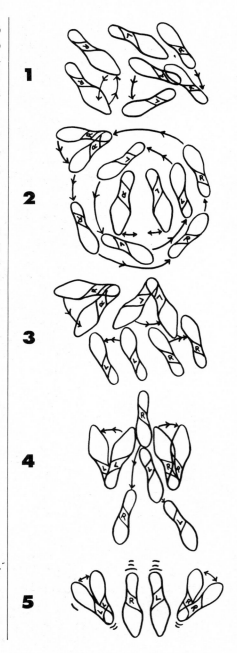

The King of The Twist was an ex-chicken plucker called Chubby Checker (né Ernest Evans; his sobriquet was said to be a tribute to Fats Domino who had named himself in tribute to Plumps Ludo who, in turn, had named himself after Dimples Backgammon).

Checker's records, 'The Twist', and its follow-up 'Let's Twist Again', started an international dance craze and spawned several movies including *Twist Around The Clock*, followed a fortnight later by *Don't Knock The Twist*; ten days later came by *Keep On Twisting*; later the same week saw *Keep On Twisting-A-Go-Go* and finally *Last Year At Marienbad* which finished shooting two days after the Twist craze had passed. The director, Alain Resnais, cut all the songs and any scenes featuring Chubby Checker, thus rendering the plot utterly meaningless. As a result, it was hailed by critics as dangerously avant garde and a seminal movie in the creation of the French Nouvelle Vague.

Before people finally stopped twisting in 1964 (or, in Belgium, in 1981), the dance had had an enormous effect on one British group who were later to record 'Twist And Shout' and who are inextricably linked with the next great instalment in the history of rock & roll. The group was, of course, Brian Poole and The Tremeloes. But, it goes without saying, that another group is even more closely associated with 'Twist And Shout'. Yes, The Isley Brothers.

But for the purposes of getting on to the next chapter it may be worth mentioning that 'Twist And Shout' was also recorded by The Beatles...

CHAPTER 6

JOHN, PAUL, GEORGE AND THE OTHER ONE

Britain had responded to the impact of rock and roll by producing stars who equalled the sexually explicit aggressivesness of Elvis Presley – stars like Billy Fury, Dickie Anger and Roddy Annoyance. And the man who was Britain's answer to Elvis Presley – when he was once asked which singer was least like him – Tommy Steele, who kicked against bourgeois convention with his scathingly biting song, 'Little White Bull'.

And now Britain was poised to lead the world with the arrival of the Swinging Sixties which, according to many started at midnight on 31st December, 1959, but, according to others didn't start until much later – one minute past midnight on 1st January, 1960. The style pioneered by groups like The Beatles would be called many things – The Beat Boom, The British Sound, The British Beat Boom, Merseybeat, Merseyboom, Merseydoates, Doseydotes, and Littlelambsidivey but most people called it The Mersey Sound.

But what exactly was The Mersey Sound? Some say it was a fusion of Tamla Motown and British Rock, others say it was the sound made by drunken seamen vomiting into the River Mersey. John Lennon had his own way of describing it, when asked what he called it, he replied: 'Arthur'. Just one example of the legendary Scouse wit which resulted in such literary masterpieces as *In His Own Write* and *A Spaniard In The Works*, which had him hailed as 'the new Lear'.[7]

John Lennon's first group was a skiffle band called The Quarrymen. Skiffle was a crude form of music that enjoyed a brief vogue in the late Fifties, it was played on such 'instruments' as washboards and The Tea Chest Bass – made from an old tea chest into which a broom handle was inserted and from which a string was stretched. Lennon, himself, played a guitar made from wood into which a 'neck' was inserted and from which four metal strings were stretched and which he bought in a guitar shop.

By playing gigs around Liverpool, Lennon and The Quarrymen were able to earn a little money which they saved to buy better instruments. As soon as he could afford it, Lennon swapped his acoustic for an electric guitar, the washboard player swapped his washboard for an automatic twin-tub washing machine with three-heat dryer settings and the

bass player swapped his tea chest for a pair of rubber gloves, which wasn't a bad deal but effectively ended his career as a musician.[8]

John Lennon formed The Quarrymen in 1956 – which, according to some, was about the middle of the 1950s – and by 1958 the group already included Paul McCartney and George Harrison. All were highly competent musicians but Lennon was dissatisfied. His innate musical genius told him there was something missing, so he immediately recruited Stuart Sutcliffe to play bass guitar.

And yet there was still some element missing. Two months later Lennon made his next huge step forward, he changed the name of the group to The Silver Beatles. Still dissatisfied and seeking that extra missing ingredient Lennon changed the name again to The Beatles.

Two months later, and only four years after forming the group, Lennon's incredible musical acumen finally identified what was missing from The Beatles and he recruited a drummer.

With the addition of drummer Pete Best, The Beatles were poised at last for stardom, but they needed guidance and they sought it from Liverpool's top promoter, the man known to everyone as 'Mr. Liverpool' – Alun Liverpool.

[7]Some authorities say this is a reference to Edward Lear, the writer of nonsense rhymes. Others that Lennon was more like King Lear, who suffered from senile dementia and went completely mad. Others really couldn't give a toss.

[8]Tragically, he later became a member of Bucks Fizz.

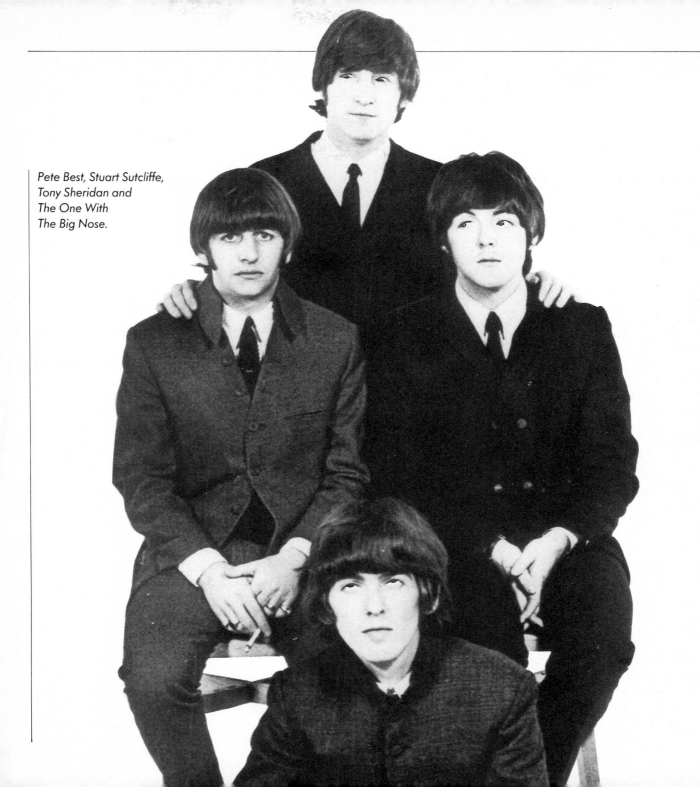

Pete Best, Stuart Sutcliffe,
Tony Sheridan and
The One With
The Big Nose.

> *I saw The Beatles playing in The Cavern and I knew exactly what to tell them. My advice was: 'Go to Hamburg'. It was time we got our own back on the Germans for what they did to us in the Second World War.*

The Beatles went to Hamburg.

HAMBURG

Hamburg today is much as it was in 1960, the largest sea port in Germany, with a population of 1,648,800 and the centre of the European vice trade. Every conceivable type of vice can be found in Hamburg, along with most other hardware lines, all of which can be freely bought in Germany's largest Do-It-Yourself superstore.

Interestingly, The Beatles never went to the superstore because they were playing in the notorious Reeperbahn, infamous the world over for its drug peddlers and prostitutes. The Beatles played in Reeperbahn clubs for eight hours every night and, having had a very good time playing with prostitutes, they then performed on stage.

It was in Hamburg that The Beatles got invaluable experience in the most fundamental skills of their trade – sex and drugs. They also played quite a lot of rock & roll and were soon spotted by a young singer called Tony Sheridan who invited them to join him on a record that was typical of the powerful, driving rock of the time, an ancient Scottish folk song called 'My Bonnie'.

In the normal course of events 'My Bonnie' would have been utterly forgotten, but back in Liverpool something very interesting was happening . . .

LIVERPOOL

On 1st October 1961 – the day, according to some when The Swinging Sixties really began – an attractive teenage boy walked into the NEMS record store in Liverpool, run by an elegant, sensitive, bachelor called Brian Epstein. The boy asked Epstein if he had a copy of a record called 'My Bonnie' made by a group called 'The Beetles'.[9]

Epstein said he hadn't got the disc but he'd try to order it and asked the boy to return that evening.

The boy returned at the appointed time and Epstein told him he hadn't managed to trace the record but asked him whether he fancied 'a bijou drinkie-poo' at a little place round the corner. The boy declined his invitation, kneed Epstein in the groin and walked out of the store and, indeed, out of the story.

Meanwhile back in . . .

HAMBURG

Stuart Sutcliffe decides to stay in Germany while the rest of The Beatles start packing to return to . . .

LIVERPOOL

. . . where, on 10th October, 1961, Epstein has stocked several copies of 'My Bonnie' and is surprised to find that they sell like hot cakes. This leads Epstein to a crucial decision: should he now switch to selling hot cakes, or should he continue in the record business?

Epstein plumps for the latter and decides to find out more about The Beatles by travelling to . . .

BELGIUM

. . . where he discovers they have yet to hear of Elvis Presley so he moves on to . . .

HAMBURG

. . . but The Beatles have left and are now in . . .

LIVERPOOL

. . . where they are playing in The Cavern.

Epstein returns to Liverpool, having spent two months trying to find The Beatles on the Reeperbahn.[10]

In November, 1961, Epstein makes his first visit to The Cavern where he sees The Beatles. He is instantly struck by John Lennon and offers to handle him.[11]

That night Brian Epstein becomes their manager and 'The Fifth Beatle'.

Epstein's first act as manager is to persuade The Beatles to take their clothes off. His second act is to assure them that he merely wants them to exchange their filthy jeans and black leather jackets for some smart collarless suits. His third act as manager is to persuade a record company to sign The Beatles. And to do that, Epstein travels to . . .

CARLISLE

A completely wasted journey as not one major record company is based in the town. Realising his mistake, Epstein then travels to . . .

---

[9] Before they achieved fame The Beatles' name was frequently mispronounced.
[10] Although he failed to find The Beatles, he did discover a great deal of other talent on the Reeperbahn. But that has nothing to do with this story.
[11] Some say that Epstein was struck by Lennon after offering to handle him.

LONDON

In January, 1962, Epstein started doing the rounds of the record companies. He was turned down by Decca and three others in quick succession but eventually found a record company executive who was prepared to listen to his tapes, hear his

George Martin, producer of the Beatles.[12]

hopes and aspirations and take him out for intimate little dinners at a chi-chi restaurant in Hampstead. But that's another story.

On the business front, he met George Martin, a senior producer at Parlophone who gave The Beatles an audition, decided to sign them and as a result became 'The Sixth Beatle'. George Martin.

In the meantime, however, The Beatles had met Sam 'Friend To All The Stars' Chuck:–

"*I remember I was in The Cavern, in Liverpool, in England, in Europe, one day and Paul McCartney came up to me and he said,* 'Mr. Chuck, we want to be the biggest beat combo in the history of the world'. And I said to him, 'Brush your hair forward, buy yourselves suits without collars and record a song called "Love Me Do".' Paul said, 'Thank you Mr. Chuck, we'll do that.' And then I said, 'And fire your drummer.' And that's what they did and that's how they became the biggest beat combo in the history of the world.* **"**

Pete 'The Fourth Beatle' Best was sacked and replaced by the drummer from Rory Storme and The Tempests. The man who became 'The Seventh Beatle' was born Richard Starkey but was soon known throughout the world as The One with The Big Nose . . .

---

[12]All right, this is George Michael, but we were worried that younger readers might be tempted to skip this extremely interesting bit.

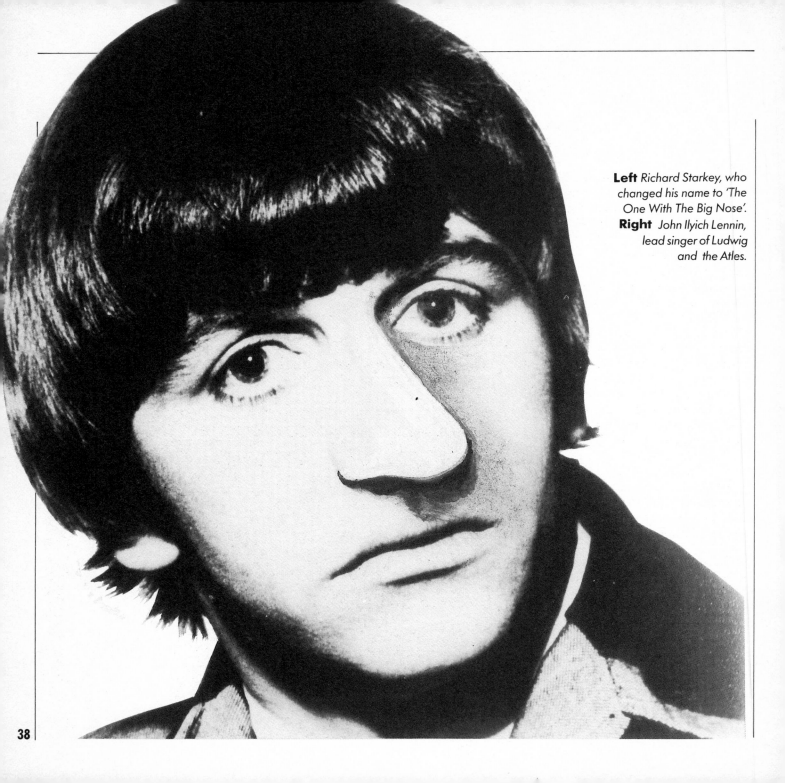

Left *Richard Starkey, who changed his name to 'The One With The Big Nose'.* **Right** *John Ilyich Lennin, lead singer of Ludwig and the Atles.*

CHAPTER 7

ENGLAND SWINGS LIKE A PENDULUM DO

Yes, in the early Sixties England really did swing like a pendulum done. Many date the start of The Swinging Sixties to 5th October, 1962, when John, Paul, George and The One With The Big Nose released their first record, 'Love Me Do'.

Almost exactly a year later Britain was in the grip of Beatlemania. It started on 13th October, 1963 – which for others was the date when The Swinging Sixties really began. That was the day the British Press finally recognised what the teenagers of Britain had known for a year: The Beatles were the biggest group in Britain. The Press instantly dubbed them 'The Mop Tops'[13] 'The Fab Four' or, catchiest of all, 'The Beatles, a popular beat combo'.

Everywhere The Beatles went, there were hysterical scenes, something that made life very difficult for the other acts who toured with them as roadie, Harry Dann, who became known as 'The Eighth Beatle', remembers well:–

"*It was very hard for the other groups to make themselves heard above all the screaming, shouting and crying. In the end I had to tell Ringo to shut up and assured him that the others didn't hate him just because he had a big nose.* "**

Beatlemania did more than just focus attention on the Beatles, it also drew people's attention to Liverpool as a centre of

[13] Except for The One With The Big Nose who was known as 'Bucket Head'.

musical excellence. And at the centre of that centre was The Cavern, a small centrally-heated club near the centre of Liverpool which became central to British pop. It also became a magnet for every record producer, agent and manager.

In that dark little basement Brian Epstein signed Priscilla White, the club's hat check girl, who changed her name and her nose to become Cilla Black. Another manager, Morrie Schlemiel, signed two waiters and a barman. Agent Dick Adams signed up Morrie Schlemiel. And entrepreneur, Adam Dicks, set up office in the gentlemen's toilet where he signed up three plainsclothes policemen. They got a five year contract and he got 12 months in Pentonville Prison.

The biggest talent spotter was, of course, Epstein who, in addition to The Beatles and Cilla 'The Ninth Beatle' Black also signed Billy J. 'The Tenth Beatle' Kramer (and his Dakotas), Gerry 'The Eleventh Beatle' Marsden (and his Pacemakers) and The Fourmost, known as 'The Twelfth-to-Fifteenth Beatles Inclusive'.

Everyone signed by Epstein benefited from a Lennon and McCartney song and virtually everyone had a hit. Everyone, that is except Tommy Ridley:–

"I could've been 'The Sixteenth Beatle'. In 1963 Brian was signing up about 12 acts a day and he had this streamlined system: you turned up at NEMS and you went to the first office where you got your contract, then you went to the second office where you got your suit – Brian insisted that we all wore nice suits on stage. Then you went to the last office where you got your hit song by John and Paul. You'd see all these kids coming out of NEMS clutching their contract, suit and song. And all of them became stars. Except me.

The day I was signed, John and Paul had popped out to do some shopping and they got behind with writing the hit songs.

So I got two suits instead. Nice suits they were, but you can't sing a suit, can you? Anyway, I took them home, got my Mum to sew collars on them and flogged them down at the market.

No regrets, though. I've made a good living running a suit stall. In fact, it's right next to the junk stall run by Billy J. Kramer."

Within a very few years the Beatles had conquered Europe, subjugated America, ignored Belgium, swept through Asia and

laid waste to Australia. The Fab Four became the three most famous men in the world and some people had also heard of The One With The Big Nose.

In 1967 they produced 'Sgt. Pepper's Lonely Hearts Club Band', a record which has been described as 'their masterwork', 'the greatest achievement in popular music' and 'a round, flat piece of vinyl with a hole in the middle'.

The release of 'Pepper' showed the new direction The Beatles were taking: their songs had become longer, broader, deeper, wider, and higher. Mostly because The Beatles were also getting higher or, at least, that's what the B.B.C. thought because it

Left *Ringo marries Maureen*
Below *The first to fourteenth Beatles inclusive.*

banned two tracks – 'A Day In The Life' and 'Lucy In The Sky With Diamonds' – which, it claimed, contained drug references. Dr Fitzgerald:–

❝ *Both songs were clearly written under the influence of L.S.D., Not Lysergic Acid Diethylamide, but pounds, shillings and pence. Lennon and McCartney were receiving so much money that they started thinking they had something important to say on this LP. Completely deluded, of course. Probably because they were taking so many drugs.* **❞**

After the triumph of 'Pepper', The Beatles began to change: led by George Harrison they found an interest in the teachings of the Maharishi Yogi Mahesh who initiated them into such Eastern mysteries as Transcendental Meditation, Transcendental Levitation and Transcendental Donation – which involved going into a hypnotic trance and giving him all their money. But one mystery was never explained – how and why four perfectly sensible people could be taken in by this giggling charlatan.

Despite the others' disillusion with mysticism, George Harrison continued his search for God with dire consequences to his music. Inevitably, people were led to ask if: 'My Sweet Lord' was really a product of divine inspiration, could The Chiffons (who had a hit with the earlier and identical 'He's So Fine') sue God for infringement of copyright?

John marries the Maharishi

By the end of the decade, cracks were becoming apparent in the group – John and Paul were taking different musical directions, George was taking religious instruction and The One With The Big Nose was taking drumming lessons. But it was too late. By the start of The Seventies a split was inevitable.

Who, ultimately, was responsible for the break-up of The Beatles? Some blamed Paul's insistence on bringing in financial advisers, others blamed The One With The Big Nose because he was the smallest. But most experts agree that the person mostly responsible was The Little Japanese Woman With The Squeaky Voice.

Whatever is said about The Little Japanese Woman With The Squeaky Voice, there's no doubt she had an extraordinary effect on Lennon, influencing him to work for peace[14] and inspiring him to write what became his most enduring song, 'Imagine'.

There are those who criticise 'Imagine' as being naive and simplistic, but surely only a towering genius could persuade others to 'imagine no possessions' while himself possessing unimaginable wealth.

Since his tragic death, Lennon has become something of a legend, his memory kept alive by The Little Japanese Woman With The Squeaky Voice and by documentary films showing him in his last days, enjoying the ordinary pleasures of life like baking a couple of loaves of bread and taking them out into Central Park to feed 5,000 people. However, as he always said, the Beatles weren't saints, least of all him and Paul, although that didn't stop the Pope naming himself after them.

After the split, the individual Beatles went onto greater heights. George wrote a book called *I, Me, Mine* which, apparently, had some autobiographical content and which appeared as a limited edition costing £1000 (some copies are still available at 99p in most good remainder stores). Following that success he went into film production and was responsible for such movies as Madonna's *Shanghai Surprise*.[15]

Of the Beatles only Paul McCartney didn't desert music – The One With The Big Nose was never in music – and he continued writing hits through the Seventies and Eighties.

It was in The Seventies that McCartney achieved a remarkable feat. 'Mull of Kintyre', written as a tribute to a Scottish island near his home, was the first record to sell over two million copies in Britain. All the more remarkable when you consider it is the dreariest dirge since 'The Death March'. He followed 'Mull of Kintyre' with 'Isla St. Clair', written as a tribute to a small, barren and inhospitable lump of Scottish rock who used to appear on *The Generation Game*.

By the beginning of The Eighties, McCartney's career seemed to be dipping, although he was notching up records all over the world. Mostly criminal records for drug taking and it is estimated that he spent more time in jail during this period than in the recording studio. But when he did get into the studio, he managed to come up with records such as 'Wonderful Christmas Time' and 'Pipes of Peace' which were equally criminal.

However, help was at hand in the shape of Sam 'Friend To All The Stars' Chuck:–

‘‘ *One day I was forging my tax returns when Paul McCartney turned up and said, 'I need your help with my career.' And I said: 'What you need to do is make a duet with Stevie Wonder and you'll be top of the charts again.' And he said, 'Thanks very much, Mr. Chuck, I'll do that.' And that's what he did.* **’’**

The result of his collaboration with Stevie Wonder was 'Ebony & Ivory' which had some profound things to say about racial harmony. Like, for example it doesn't matter what colour a person is because underneath the skin everyone is basically a piano.

In The Eighties McCartney also went into film production. *Give My Regards To Broad Street* was described in the press, on radio and television as 'A masterpiece' and 'Probably the finest cinematic achievement ever'. However, not everyone agreed with Paul McCartney. The film suffered the indignity of being released on video 24 hours before its cinema premiere and critics were not impressed by a movie in which the star spends a day and a night rushing around Britain in a desperate attempt to find the one vital element that's gone missing – the plot.

The break-up of The Beatles[16] was the end of an era. Millions mourned the loss of The Greatest Rock & Roll Band In The World. But some of their contemproaries kept rocking into The Eighties. And, indeed, into their eighties . . .

---

[14] See 'the Years Of Change'. A very dull footnote. Sorry.
[15] The surprise being that it was ever released.
[16] Little has subsequently been heard of The One With The Big Nose, although there are rumours that he's a huge star in Belgium.

CHAPTER 8

THE OLDEST ROCK & ROLL BAND IN THE WORLD

The Rolling Stones were the antithesis of The Beatles. It's difficult to see how the two groups could have been more dissimilar. The Beatles came from Liverpool, The Stones didn't. There were four Beatles and five Stones. Nobody in the Stones was called George Harrison. And The Stones didn't have The One With The Big Nose. They had The One With The Big Lips.

His name was Mick Jagger and, astonishingly, nearly thirty years later, it still is, But so much else has changed in that time. For a start, four of those five rebellious Stones are nearly thirty years older, but despite their age they still take delight in shocking. They perform shocking concerts, give shocking interviews and make shocking records. And Bill Wyman still has sex with young girls less than half his age – including one or two who are barely into their thirties.

What is incredible is that The Stones have kept rolling despite the death of their leader Brian Jones. And what's even more incredible is that the Stones have kept rolling despite the fact that Keith Richard has had more drugs than I.C.I. Perhaps most incredible of all is the fact that Keith Richard IS still alive.

The Rolling Stones are, arguably, The Best Rock & Roll Band In The World. But they are, incontestably, The Oldest Rock & Roll Band In The World. Asked in 1983 whether they didn't find touring a strain at their age, Mick Jagger said it was slightly easier since Bill Wyman had

Above *Mick Jagger enjoys a Mars bar.*
Right *Marianne Faithfull enjoys a Mars bar.*

received his Senior Citizen's bus pass but that they'd be doing less touring as it became increasingly difficult to get Wyman on stage and to stop Keith Richard falling off it.

From the start The Rolling Stones set out to offend with their clothes, their songs, their attitude and their behaviour. In 1963 Jagger, Wyman and Jones were convicted of insulting behaviour for urinating against a wall. And even today members of the group think nothing of entering public toilets and defecating into them.

In the Sixties The Stones became the symbol of rebelliousness; everywhere they went they caused offence with their threat-ening behaviour, their foul language and their blatant promiscuity and they were no better off stage.

They were The Bad Boys of Rock – there were the sex scandals, the drug arrests, the riots everywhere they went, all of which culminated in the biggest outrage of all, on 22nd January, 1967 – the date when, for many, The Swinging Sixties stopped – and the day that became known as:

BLACK SUNDAY!

This was the day they appeared on Britain's top-rated television show, *Sunday Night At The London Palladium*. In front of an audience of nine million appalled viewers they committed the grossest, vilest and most offensive insult of all – at the end of the show they refused to climb onto the revolving stage and wave bye-bye.

It was fearless gestures like this that made them the symbol of youthful revolt. No other group represented the sex-and-drugs-and-rock-&-roll-and-not-waving-bye-bye lifestyle more outrageously than The Stones.

But perhaps the most notorious incident occurred when Keith Richard's home was raided by the police and Mick Jagger was charged with being in possession of a Mars bar and eating it in a manner – and in a Marianne – liable to cause offence.

The Stones' raunchy reputation preceded them to The States and caused a certain amount of trepidation. Before their

Daily Mirror

4d Saturday, March 18, 1967 No 19,667

'Stones' get summonses after raid

JAGGER IS ACCUSED OVER DRUGS

BY BARRY STANLEY and JOHN SANDFORD

TWO of the Rolling Stones pop group—Mick Jagger and Keith Richard—have been accused of offences against the drug laws.

Summonses against the two men—both aged
police raid on Richard's £20,000 ho

appearance on *The Ed Sullivan Show* they
received this telegram:

CANNOT ALLOW YOU TO SING 'LET'S SPEND
THE NIGHT TOGETHER' STOP LYRICS TOO
SUGGESTIVE STOP PLEASE CHANGE
THE WORDS STOP REGARDS STOP

                    ED SULLIVAN

Ed Sullivan replied:

IF YOU DON'T CHANGE THE WORDS
YOU WON'T APPEAR ON THE SHOW

                    SULLIVAN

The Stones wired back:

YOU CAN'T STOP US STOP
WE WON'T BE STOPPED STOP
MUST STOP SAYING STOP STOP

ROLLING STOPS SORRY STONES STOP

HOW ABOUT 'LET'S SPEND THE EVENING
TOGETHER'?

                    ROLLING STONES

NO, STILL TOO SUGGESTIVE

SULLIVAN

SUGGEST 'LET'S SPEND SOME TIME TOGETHER IN THE NEAR FUTURE WITHOUT HAVING ANY PHYSICAL CONTACT WHATSOEVER'

It was typical of The Stones' uncompromising attitude that they replied with a single, four-letter word:

HOW ABOUT 'LET'S SPEND PART OF THE AFTERNOON TOGETHER?

ROLLING STONES

OKAY

As a result of their appearance on *The Ed Sullivan Show,* The Stones took America by storm. But meanwhile, back in Britain . . .

CHAPTER 9

ENGLAND STILL SWUNG LIKE A PENDULUM DONE

By 1965, which for many was when The Swinging Sixties really started, the centre of the universe had swung from Liverpool to London. London was where it was at. London was 'fab', it was 'gear', it was gravy.[17] The whole metropolis was throbbing with creativity: photographers, models, musicians, designers and actors were emerging from the crooks and nannies of the city.[18]

It was in London that a designer called Jim Gordon invented The Mini. He had the brilliant idea of making a compact engine and setting it transversely across a short wheel-based chassis. Within a year, 20 million Minis were being produced in a huge variety of colours and styles. Unfortunately, they were incredibly uncomfortable to wear, causing 'dolly birds' to suffer from metal fatigue, so he went back to the drawing board and turned his design into a range of cheap little cars.

It was left to Mary Quant to come up with the even more brilliant idea of producing them in soft, alluring fabrics and so the Mini Skirt was born.

The Mini Skirt was worn by all the trendiest 'dolly birds' like Lesley Hornby, known to all as 'Twiggy'; Jean Shrimpton, known to all as 'The Shrimp'; and of course, Kathy Parsons, known to all as 'The Prawn', who in a profile in *The Sun-*

Christine Keeler who brought down a Conservative government by wearing a skirt two inches above her knees.

day *Times Colour Supplement*, recalled her days of hectic fame:

"*I remember everything was so frantic! I was just rushing around the whole time from art galleries to recording to television studios to photographers studios, and then back to the art galleries before starting all over again. I was just so busy!*

What did you actually do?

Nothing, really, I was just famous.[19] **"**

MODS AND ROCKERS

British youth of the day was split into two factions called Mods and Rockers who dressed in their own distinctive styles.

Mods were the smarter of the two, they loved parkas, Vespas, Lambrettas and any other type of Italian food.

The Rockers wore winkle-picker shoes, tight jeans and leather jackets with polished studs. Every Saturday night the Mods and the Rockers would dress themselves with great care, groom their hair so that not a strand was out of place, go on the town and beat the shit out of each other.[20]

[17]This is a mospirnt. Sorry, misprint. It should read 'groovy'.
[18]This is not a misprint. In the Sixties anyone could become a star, especially crooks and nannies.
[19]Kathy Parsons was known as 'The Prawn' because she had the I.Q. of a crustacean. She later became a Conservative M.P.
[20]In the late-Seventies there were two very similar youth factions called Rods And Mockers. Rods dressed up to look like Rod Stewart and the far larger group, The Mockers, used to take the piss out of them for looking like prats.

Right *Early version of the mini skirt with obvious design faults.*

The clashes between Mods and Rockers originally took place on Bank Holidays in seaside resorts such as Margate, Clacton and Brighton. Then, as they grew older and wealthier, they would organise day trips to Boulogne and long weekends in Paris. Now, as they've reached middle age, they go on fortnight package holidays to Tenerife and beat the shit out of each other.

Back in the Sixties THE Mod band was The Who, arguably The Best But One Rock & Roll Band In The World, The Who survived into the 80s to become, incontestably, The Second Oldest Rock & Roll Band In The World.

The Who comprised of vocalist Roger Daltrey, with Pete Townshend on lead guitar, John Entwistle on bass and Keith Moon on drugs. The presiding genius of the group was Townshend who summed up the philosophy of the young in his song 'My Generation'. In it Townshend declared: 'Hope to die before I get old.' But, tragically, he lived to be a middle-aged millionaire. Such are the cruel tricks played by the whirligig of time.

The Who sprang to notoriety because they smashed their instruments on stage. But, as Pete Townshend explained to the authors:

Below *Glue sniffing the Townshend way.*

66 *We never intended to smash the instruments, it was all an accident. I used to have this trick of whirling my arm around and one night I accidentally hit Keith's drums, they fell onto John Entwistle who dropped his guitar onto the stage and . . .* [21] 99

The Who's greatest hour came on 15th August, 1966 – the day that, many claim, truly marks the start of The Swinging Sixties – when they played their biggest gig to 100,000 people at The Dallas Megadrome.

And, as usual, their performance brought the house down (see picture, right).

When not demolishing the world's largest venues, there were legendary stories about The Who – stories of wrecked hotel rooms, where all the furniture was broken up and ten people were found in the same bed. But we're not concerned with the problems they encountered when over-booked on a Spanish package holiday, we're concerned with the Permissive Society which was then at its erotic height.

[21] The interview was discontinued as Townshend accidentally broke his chair, smashed into a lamp and trod on the tape recorder.

CHAPTER 10

SEX & SEX & ROCK & ROLL & SEX

Yes The Sixties were swinging like an orgiastic pendulum. Everyone was indulging in Free Love.[22] The young were urged to 'do their own thing' and 'let it all hang out'.

The songs of the time echoed the new sexual frankness. Pete Townshend was instrumental in broadening the scope of the pop song, turning it from happy-go-lucky dance music into a form of expression that could deal with larger, more adult and often controversial subjects that reflected the rise of The Permissive Society. He broke taboos with 'Pictures Of Lily', the first song that was overtly about masturbation. Later The Kinks' record 'Lola' dealt with the transvesticism and the last barrier was finally breached when Rolf Harris openly sung of homosexuality in 'Two Little Boys'.

One of the manifestations of the new promiscuity was The Groupie, a girl who offered sex to rock stars. This presented unique problems to members of the road crew, as roadie Dick Trent recalls:

" *It was almost a full time job just keeping the groupies away from the stars. I mean, it wasn't what I was employed to do. I just did it to annoy the band.* **"**

One of the most notorious – and, indeed, popular – groupies who constantly managed to get past the minders was Lindy Black who claims to have slept with most of the biggest pop stars of the Sixties including a Stone, a Yardbird, a Who, two Troggs, three Swinging Blue Jeans and a

Hermit who, as a result, was forced to renounce his religious vows. She also says she had several Kinks before enjoying a long relationship with an Animal.[23]

Lindy recalls one encounter she had in London's Ad Lib Club in 1967:

" *I was sitting at a table when a very famous rock star – I won't mention any names – came over and introduced himself. Five minutes later we were screwing ourselves senseless right there, under the table. Five minutes! Must be my record! Mind you, there wasn't really anything else to do. I mean, have you ever tried talking to a rock star?* **"**

The group that had the most loyal female fans was, of course, The Beatles. Women flocked round them and were so fanatical in their devotion that some even slept with The One With The Big Nose, including Lindy who remembers:

" *Was he good in bed? Let's just say I didn't get a wink's sleep all night. My God, you should have heard the noise he made! I've never heard anyone like him. But, of course, I've never slept with anyone with such an enormous one before. I mean, that nose! When he snored the whole house shook.* **"**

---

[22]Everyone, that is, except the authors. Two of whom were too young. The other doesn't have that excuse. Unfortunately.

[23]Lindy Black never revealed which Animal. But, judging from certain Swedish movies that have fallen into the authors' hands it seems to have been a large Doberman Pinscher.

The launch party of this book. (For Christ's sake don't use this!)

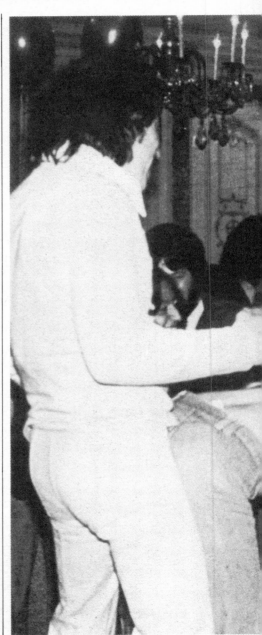

Jim Morrison: an inspiration to the young.

One of The Beatles' most persistent fans was Emma Landis:

" *I sat outside John Lennon's house for five years. And it was worth it because one day John himself, personally, drove over my foot as he came out of his gate.*

Of course, I never talked to him. We had sex together, but I never actually got to talk to him. **"**

Mick Jagger had one of the raunchiest reputations in rock. A reputation confirmed by Dick Trent, one of The Stones' roadies:

" *When we were on the road Mick used to go everywhere with a book full of telephone numbers. It was incredible, wherever he was he'd just open the book and find the number he wanted. In fact, I've kept a page from it as a souvenir . . .* **"**

" *He could get anyone he wanted – furniture upholsterers, commodity brokers, wholesale tobacconists and purveyors of smokers' requisites – at any time of the day or night.* **"**

Amazingly, Jagger's reputation as a stud is exceeded by that of Bill Wyman who claims to have slept with over a thousand women. When we asked Wyman what sex was like in The Sixties, he shook his head, sobbed quietly and said it wasn't as good as it had been in his Forties and Fifties.

The new sexual liberation of The Swinging Sixties was reflected in the stage acts of various performers. The sexual posturing of one rock star, Jim Morrison of The Doors, made international headlines:

Jim Morrison: a hardened criminal.

POLICE DEPT
NEW HAVEN CONN
23750
12·10·67

At a concert in Miami in 1969 he went too far and exposed himself before 20,000 people. He was arrested, charged with obscenity and indecent exposure but the charges were later dropped when an F.B.I. spokesman explained:

" *It was a lot of fuss about such a little thing.* **"**

Perhaps the most sexually outrageous performer of all was Jimi Hendrix as a member of his road crew, Bob Laker, remembers:

" *Let's be honest, Jimi made love to his guitar. I used to watch him some nights and there he was, screwing his guitar. I mean, Jimi had a hell of a reputation as a ladies' man but the truth is he really had the hots for guitars.* **"**

The tradition of such sexual antics continues to this day. Prince has certainly been influenced by Hendrix. On stage he does extraordinary and lubricious things with his guitar, including caressing it, licking it, grinding it into his groin, simulating oral sex with it and, most offensive of all, actually playing it.

But back in 1966, Prince was still 20 years in the future – one of the major charms of that year – and as '66 turned in '67, the Years of Promiscuity were soon to become The Years of Change.[25]

[24] Jim Exposes Himself.
[25] See heading of next chapter.

55

CHAPTER 11

THE YEARS OF CHANGE[26]

The second half of The Sixties were the years of change. So rapid was the change in these changing years that within a mere 12 months 1966 had changed into 1967. No year saw greater change than 1967. It was the year of Peace and Love summed up by Scott McKenzie's worldwide hit 'San Francisco'.

Dressed in a kaftan, be-decked with beads and bells and wearing flowers in his hair, Scott McKenzie looked a complete prat. Nevertheless, he and the rest of the psychedelic hippies believed that through rock music, drugs and free love, they could change the world. They had the innocence of children and the I.Q. of a duvet.

They called themselves The Flower Children. Their slogan was 'Make Love, Not War' and they took their message to military establishments all over Britain and America until the authorities banned them because of increased violence as soldiers fought each other over whose turn it was to make love to a Flower child.

The Flower Children had their own anthems in the summer of '67, Songs like 'A Whiter Shade Of Pale' by a group which, until that year had been an unsuccessful beat combo called The Paramounts. Under the influence of peace, love and mind expanding drugs, they borrowed a Latin tag and called themselves Procol Harum. Some considered them the future of rock, other considered them a bunch of pretentious bastards.

The Hippies of San Francisco believed in Free Love, a philosophy that was opposed by most moral and religious leaders and all prostitutes whose business was being ruined.

In the Haight-Ashbury district of San Francisco, when they weren't taking drugs or bonking their brains out, the Hippies demonstrated vigorously for Peace until neighbours complained about the appalling noise they were making.

The people who led The Peace Movement were John Lennon and The Little Japanese Woman With The Squeaky Voice.[27]

There was nothing these two wouldn't do for Peace, nowhere they wouldn't go (except Belgium). They worked tirelessly for Peace.

The planted acorns for Peace.

The sat in canvas bags for Peace.

The booked into expensive hotels for Peace.

And, with inexhaustible energy, they lay around in bed for Peace.

The Hippies wanted to change the world. Many subscribed to John Lennon's vision of changing it into a place of peace and plenty. But most wanted to change it into a large pink cocktail onion called Samantha. Such were the effects of L.S.D.[28]

While John and The Little Japanese Woman with The Squeaky Voice were sleeping for Peace, other rock stars, led by George Harrison, were looking East.

East to the Zen temples of Japan.

East to the Confucian Philosophy of China. East to the ashrams of Nepal.

East to an abbattoir in Ipswich, England, where Steve Belt, lead singer of Green Exploding Laxative found his personal road to Damascus when he was converted by one of the group members, His Holiness The Swami River (né Ted River). One day Belt was struck by The Swami's

---

[26]Told you so. See footnote 25, previous page.
[27]See Footnote 15. No, don't bother, it's very dull.
[28]Some of the stars of The Sixties became casualties of drugs. One was Brian Wilson, the genius behind the Beach Boys. According to Charlie Ronson: 'He can be compared to John Lennon and Bob Dylan. But mostly I'd compare him to a courgette. Or possibly a cauliflower. Let's face it, the man is a vegetable. With all those drugs inside him, it's no wonder he has the mental capacity of a radish. Absolutely tragic to see a man with that amount of talent reduced to ratatouille.'

vibes which he picked up and smashed over Belt's head. The Swami was a brilliant vibes player but he had a violent temper. After he had recovered, Belt journeyed to India where he sat at the feet of the Maharishi Raitha Mahesh who promised

The Flower Pot Men who had a huge hit in '67 with 'Let's go to San Francisco', pictured here with weed, who they later smoked.

to look after all his yearnings. Unfortunately, Belt misunderstood the Maharishi who had, in fact, offered to look after all his 'earnings'. When they were spent the disillusioned Belt then turned to the preachings of The Rev. Ding Bat Loon and became what he is today, a Loonie.

What were the results of the Hippies' efforts to change the world through love, peace and drugs? Many felt they had suc-

ceeded. As the Sixties gave way to the Seventies they were convinced that they'd managed to stop all wars, cure world poverty and live happily ever after. Unfortunately these were just the rambling delusions of their drug-crazed brains. The vast majority realised that sex and drugs and peace weren't having any effect so they turned to the next best things – sex and drugs and violence.

CHAPTER 12

THE YEARS OF PROTEST

In all the Years of Change no year was more changeable than 1968 which was known as THE Year of Change until that changed and it became known as The Year Of Protest.

In Chicago...hippies clashed with Mayor Daley's police.

In Tokyo...Red Brigades smashed police blockades.

In Paris...students rioted on the boulevards. And, most violent of all, in London...Manchester United's fans celebrated beating Benfica by four goals to one at Wembley.

Meanwhile, in Belgium...nothing had changed. So no change there.

THE YEAR OF ANGER

1968 was the year of anger. The year when young people finally said 'No!' in songs that voiced their bitter fury and frustration by such anti-establishment heroes as:

Des O'Connor who bitterly sang 'I Pretend'...

Cliff Richard who protested angrily with 'Congratulations'...

Louis Armstrong who raged against injustice with 'What a Wonderful World'.

No area of society was immune to the wave of revolution. The voice of protest roared through the arts, literature, politics, life-style, ornamental macramé and even rock music. And at the forefront of this protest was one man ...

... Bob Dylan, a close personal friend of John Lennon although they hardly met.

The man they called 'The Leader Of The Protest Movement' started life as Robert Zimmerman, as Sam 'Friend To All The Stars' Chuck, remembers:

"One day Robert Zimmerman came to me and said, 'Mr Chuck, I want to be The Leader Of The Protest Movement.' And I told him: 'Change your name to Bob Dylan. Then get yourself a battered old guitar, a doo-dah for holding your harmonica and, most important of all, a silly blue denim cap.' And that's what he did.[29]*"*

To some Dylan was a living legend, a prophet, an immortal. To others he was a Jewish singer who made pop records. Still others believe that Dylan started the Protest Movement single-handed when in 1962 he stood on the stage of a tiny club in Greenwich village and in his curiously nasal tones performed the first protest song. Before he'd finished the first verse, the audience was on its feet protesting. Dylan was a man who suffered for his music and then made the rest of us suffer as well.

Dylan's Protest Period was soon followed by his Meteorological Period when he wrote such songs as 'Blowin' In The Wind', 'A Hard Rain's Gonna Fall' and 'Rainy Day Women'. Dylan's songs ranted against inequality, unemployment and poverty. And have actually managed to change things like poverty by making him a millionaire.[30]

He wrote songs about every form of injustice. They were about The Bomb, about Civil Rights, about capital punishment. But, worst of all, they were about twenty minutes long.

It was left to others to have commercial hits with Dylan songs – The Byrds scored with 'Mr Tambourine Man' while in Britain Manfred Mann – a popular beat combo who had previously launched blistering attacks on society with songs like 'Doo Wah Diddy Diddy' – now made the charts with Dylan's 'If You Gotta Go, Go Now', 'Just Like A Woman' and 'Mighty Quinn'.

Manfred Mann made a fortune out of these songs, even though they never met Bob Dylan. Like many others at the time they borrowed Dylan's image, his songs and even his lawnmower.

Astonishingly, no group ever had a hit with the lawnmower although it can be heard in the background of Tom Jones's 'Green Green Grass Of Home'.

The message Dylan was putting across was 'lay down your guns and pick up a guitar'. But how practical is the idea? Perhaps, in certain circumstances – hand-to-hand combat, for instance – the guitar could be as useful as a gun. With a good swing on it and a good aim, it could inflict some pretty impressive damage to an enemy. But for long-range fighting, it's unlikely that the guitar could be of much use when compared to the Kalashnikov.

Dylan was one of the many artists who

[29]The silly blue denim cap, along with the essential battered jacket, distressed to order by craftsmen, the lovingly hand-scuffed cowboy boots and the petit-point protest badges were obtained from Austin de Lange of Savile Row, London – Bespoke Tailors To The Protest Movement And Purveyors Of Doo-Dahs By Appointment To H. M. The Queen For Over Thirty Years.
[30]Dylan's songs have also charted his own religious voyage. One minute he was an agnostic, the next he was a born again Jew. The next minute he was a born again Christian and the minute after that he was a born again agnostic again. Which just goes to show there's one born again every minute.

Cliff Richard: a tribute to the embalmer's art. (He may be celibate but he still checks everyday to see that everything's there).

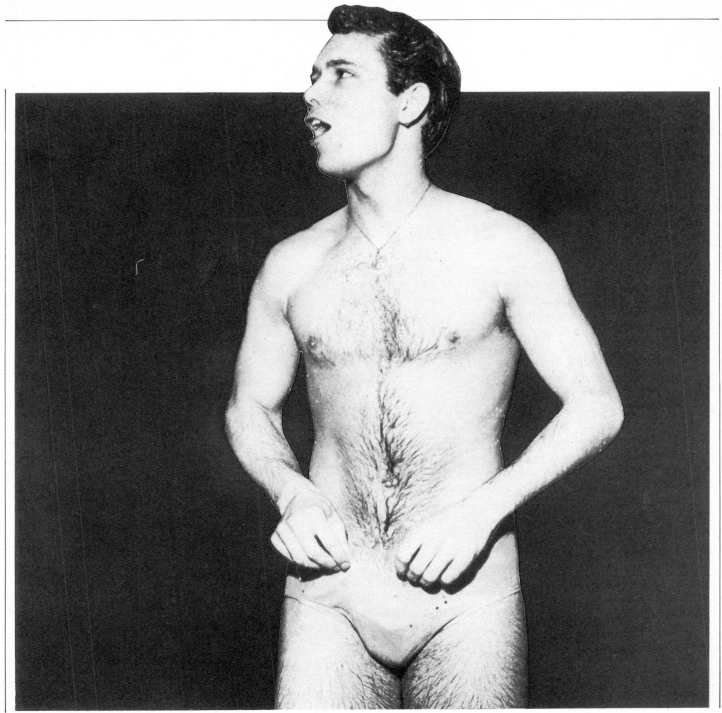

believed there was more to rock music than Awopbopaloobopalopbamboom. Over the next twenty years their voices were to be raised against the injustices of war, famine and enormous tax bills they received for singing against war and famine.

Organisations sprang up like Rock Against Racism, Rock Against The Bomb, Rock Against Apartheid, Rock Against Unemployment, Rock Against Traffic Wardens, Rock Against Doggie Doos On The Pavements and Rock Against Those Little Key Things On Sardine Cans That Always Snap When You're Trying To Open Them Causing You To Cut Your Finger.

They came to serve the cause of peace with such songs as 'Street Fighting Man' and 'Saturday Night's Alright For Fighting'.

These concerned rock stars asked pertinent questions of society like: How many roads must a man walk down before he can learn to be free? And: Does your chewing gum lose its flavour on the bedpost over night?

Regrettably, over the years, the issues have become more complicated. Once Country Joe would sing:

'Uncle Sam's got himself in a hell of a jam, Way down yonder in Viet Nam.'
More recently he'd have to sing:
'Uncle Sam's got himself in a hell of a jam with some of the extreme splinter groups of the Shi'ite Militia In East Beirut.'

No self-respecting protest singer wants to sing about wars that don't scan properly.

In Britain protest rock has become a party political issue with Red Wedge providing a focus for rock stars with social-

ist beliefs. Among the most prominent were members of The Style Council whose song, 'The Walls Come Tumbling Down', was an angry blast against the shoddy standards of building, especially of council houses. And, more especially, of Style Council houses where basic facilities like plumbing are often so ineptly installed that frequently the swimming pool and jacuzzi don't work.

There has yet to be a similar organisation aligning itself behind the Conservative Party, but there are plans for rock stars committed to the S.D.P. to release a re-make of the Steppenwolf song, 'Born To Be Wild' entitled 'Born To Be More Than A Little Concerned About The Way Things Are Going, Quite Frankly'. And on the 'B' side – 'We Shall Not Be Moved (Unless We Can Be Supplied With A Pretty good Reason For Moving, In which Case We Will Agree To Be Moved Having, We Feel, Registered Our Protest).'

But twenty years after the inception of the Protest Movement, the question remains: can rock music change anything? One man thinks it can and he maintains that rock music changed his life, turning him from a humble school teacher called Gordon into a very famous, extremely rich and sexually desirable megastar called Sting.

Meanwhile, these Years of Change were changing inexorably. No sooner had 1968 changed to 1969 than came the biggest change of all: The Sixties changed into The Seventies, A New Decade . . .

Right *The end of the angry years: young people still stroll in support of the SDP.*

I SAY,
HANG
ON A
MINUTE.

WE SHALL NOT
BE MOVED!
UNLESS WE CAN BE
SUPPLIED WITH A PTO
PRETTY GOOD REASON

CHAPTER 13

THE NINETEEN-SEVENTIES – A NEW DECADE

Yes, our story has at last brought us to the 1970s. And who can forget them? A period that bridged the 60s and the 80s in a way almost no other decade could.

The culmination of the Sixties' creation and endeavour, the Super Seventies threw up many a Star who would make us sing and many a singer who would make us throw up.

These were the Glitter Years. The years of hot pants, platform boots, nail varnish, and sequins. And for the girls – tank tops, Doc Martens and boys' haircuts. Yes the gender-bending had begun.

Glam Rock, Shock Rock, Glitter Rock. this was not so much the Rock of Ages, but the Age of Rocks.

Glitter Rock was of course named after the man who started it all, the now legendary Paul Raven, who over a period of 10 years and under his pseudonym Gary Glitter, staged 14 farewell tours, but sadly 15 revivals. But Gary was not the only subscriber to Glitter Rock. Sweet, Wizzard, T. Rex, Clifford T. Ward, and of course, the still great Queen – a group described at the time by the music press as, 'the poor man's Led Zeppelin', 'the thinking man's Pickety Witch', and 'the deaf man's Lynsey de Paul'.

Their song 'Bohemian Rhapsody', thought by many experts to be their first No. 1, is alleged to have 180 vocal tracks on it, although by recording the same voice twice, they were able to limit the number of singers required to 90. Today it still

Marc Bolan after he hit the tree.

stands as a beautifully crafted record, and lays down to make an attractive ash-tray.

One of the most outrageous performers of this era was the so-called 'Queen of the Shock Rock', Alice Cooper. His stage act included sexual antics, live snakes, and the bloody execution of a stuffed doll, and most outrageous of all, his first hit single 'School's Out' had the unthinkable audacity to openly speak out in favour of school holidays.

But the man who can justifiably claim to have spawned the Glitter Generation is someone who may nowadays be a household name, but in the early days owed a great deal to Sam Chuck 'The Friend To All The Stars', as Sam is only too happy to confess:

❝ *I remember one day Mr. Marc Bolan came up to me and said, 'I wanna be a superstar, Mr. Chuck'. And I said, 'Boy! You dye your hair red, pretend to a be a spaceman, and call yourself Ziggy Stardust. And you'll be rich and famous.' And he said, 'No thank you, Mr. Chuck.' And I said, 'O.K. I'll give the idea to David Bowie, and that's how David Bowie spawned the Glitter Generation.* **❞**

Marc Bolan himself was to become a rock and roll casualty but Charlie Ronson has a clear idea of how his career would have gone had he lived:

❝ *Well his career was on the slide at the time of his death but his song 'Telegram Sam' shows the direction he would have gone in. I think he'd have been employed to write the signature tune of* Postman Pat. **❞**

Bowie's method of constructing song lyrics was to cut up lines that he'd written and then mix them up in a random order. It was a controversial technique and not without its problems, as this first attempt shows:

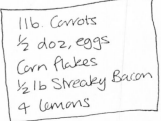

1lb. Carrots
½ doz, eggs
Corn Flakes
½ lb Streaky Bacon
4 Lemons

Realising a shopping list was not the ideal raw material, Bowie turned his attention to newspaper cuttings, with little more success.

Tonight's Forecast

Vice girls gets five years

He then tried the same technique, writing poetry first. But sadly it was to result in equally meaningless gibberish:

Ashes to Ashes, Funk to Flunky
We all know Major Tom's a junkie

David Bowie in one of his many guises, this time as "the man with the bad teeth".

Bowie's stage acts in the early 70s had to be seen to be believed. His training as a mime artist and in particular his ability to remain in one position for a long time without saying anything, stood Bowie in good stead for his later career as an actor.

His first film, *The Man Who Failed To Earth* was at the time a critical success. And indeed people have continued to criticise its success ever since. For his next excursion into the acting world, he turned to Bertold Brecht. Unfortunately, however, Brecht was dead, and so he turned instead to the B.B.C., who by a happy coincidence were about to shoot a play Brecht had written before his death. Bowie took the leading part in *Baal* and refused to give it back. The effect of his performance on the televison audience was extraordinary. And many of them never woke up.

SUPER HEROES OF THE SUPER 70s

Eric 'Slowhand' Clapton: so-called because he got a slow hand-clap every time he played. Arguably the first of the great guitar superheroes.

Jimmy 'Second Hand' Page: so-called because he played a guitar he bought second-hand from Eric Clapton. Arguably the second of the great guitar superheroes.

Rick 'Two Hands' Wakeman: so-called because of the number of hands he used to play the piano. Arguably ineligible for the title, great superhero.

Bjorn 'Back-Hand' Borg: so-called because of his incredible skill with a tennis racket. Arguably, nothing to do with rock.

SUPER GROUPS OF THE SUPER 70s

The Super guitar heroes of the Super 70s led the way for a new pop phenomenon: the Supergroup.

Supergroups were formed when individual musicians started believing they were far too good to play in the bands that had made them famous, left them in the lurch and pissed off to play with a bunch of other big heads.

Arguably the first Supergroup was Blind Faith. Put together the guitar genius of Eric Clapton, the drumming of Ginger Baker, the voice of Stevie Windwood and the bass playing of Ric Grech, and what have you got? Enough conflicting opinions to ensure the group splits up within 6 months of forming.

BLOOPERGROUP

And as well as the attempts to form the best-ever band, there was also the attempts to form the worst-ever band. The man responsible for the ill-fated project was a certain London impresario, Daniel Goldburg of Promovision.

" *First off, we managed to get Peter Tork of the Monkees on guitar, which was a pretty good start. Then I managed to sign The One With The Big Nose from The Beatles on drums. Then I decided to get that French puff on keyboards. What's his face? Richard Clayderman, that's him. Then we got Nick Berry on vocals – enough said. And just to fill it out a bit, I put that tall gangly bint from* Fame *in to play the cello. As you can imagine, they only made one record. Bloody horrible, it was. Sold well in Belgium though.* **"**

SUPER-SUPERGROUPS OF THE SUPER 70s

From the Supergroups of the 70s emerged the Super-Supergroups – bands who would attempt to outdo each other in their use of complicated technical wizardry on stage.

Peter Gabriel, lead singer of Genesis, would dress up in a vast triangular, electronic head-dress in 'Watcher of the Skies', and as an enormous sunflower in his portrayal as Narcissus. That was until he was committed to Stanley Mental Hospital in 1973.

Pink Floyd, not to be outdone, had a plane flying over the audience and crashing into the foot of the stage as their finale. That is until the Civil Aviation Authority put a stop to it after the passenger death toll had got out of hand.[32]

And Rick Wakeman dressed in a gold lamé cloak had two huge plastic dinosaurs fighting a battle to the death, as he played 'Journey To The Centre Of The Earth'. He now shares a room with Peter Gabriel.

The Super-Supergroups led the way for many other forms of rock. First there was Underground Rock: so-called because most of the bands had begun by busking in Tube stations, before being thrown out when people complained they couldn't hear the trains above the row they were making.

Next came Progressive Rock: so-called because the bands started playing one chord, and it was a good 40 minutes before

---

[32] However, Gary Numan imitated this in the Eighties.

The sensible Seventies: Peter Gabriel and Rick Wakeman performing in Stanley hospital.

they had progressed to a second.

And finally there was Classical Rock, pioneered by Keith Emerson, a musician who approached the classics with all the reverence and subtlety of a pain-maddened rhino with haemorrhoids.

SUPER-SUPERGROUPS OF THE SUPER SUPER 70s

Standing head and shoulders above the rest of the Supergroups of this era, is a handful of mega Super-Doopa Supergroups whose careers and record success were tied in with extensive television series. Who can forget them:

The Wombles, the Archies, and latterly the Smurfs, were all masterminded

The effect of too much grass on rock groups.

by the same man, a Dutchman, one Jan Kirschler. We went over to his new home in Santa Fe, New Mexico, and shot him.

An interview in the New Melody Mirror at the time of the Archie's split shows some of the tensions within the group . . .

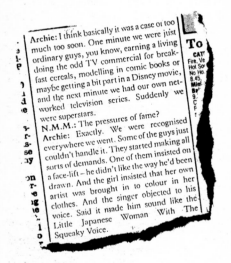

Archie: I think basically it was a case of too much too soon. One minute we were just ordinary guys, you know, earning a living doing the odd TV commercial for breakfast cereals, modelling in comic books or maybe getting a bit part in a Disney movie, and the next minute we had our own networked television series. Suddenly we were superstars.

N.M.M.: The pressures of fame?

Archie: Exactly. We were recognised everywhere we went. Some of the guys just couldn't handle it. They started making all sorts of demands. One of them insisted on a face-lift – he didn't like the way he'd been drawn. And the girl insisted that her own artist was brought in to colour in her clothes. And the singer objected to his voice. Said it made him sound like the Little Japanese Woman With The Squeaky Voice.

And of course the Seventies were dominated by two other family groups – the Osmonds and the Jacksons who were living proof of the benefits of contraception.

THE MID-SEVENTIES

Our journey through the unfolding pages of time has brought us to the opening of a new era. An era that will reveal the joys and tragedy, the turmoil and turbulence, the heights and depths, the tos and fros, the sixes and sevens, and the Marks and Spen-

Top *Abba.*

Right *Brotherhood of Man.*

cers of the world of Rock Music. The Mid-Seventies were years that started in the middle of the decade in 1975 – a time when music was either wonderful or awful, or somewhere in between. In short, an era that was frighteningly similar to almost every other era. But they were also the years of M.O.R. or Middle Of The Road music, and A.O.R. or All Over The Road music, sometimes known as Abba Orientated Rock.[33].

Abba proved that even people as tediously suicidal (and indeed as suicidally tedious) as the Swedes could dominate the world music scene.[34] Their success gave rise to a number of similar half boy, half girl outfits, culminating most recently, of course, in Duran Duran. The man responsible for many of the 70s clones was businessman Barney Wood:

❝ *We basically had to make sure no-one would recognise the similarity between Abba and the clones. So we hit upon this idea for the first of them, The Brotherhood of Man, that would make them totally different from Abba. We gave one of them a moustache. That way no-one would make the connection and in addition, their attention would be distracted by the sight of a woman with a moustache.* **❞**

DISCO!

Yes, this was also the age of 'D.I.S.C.O.' – disco films, disco clothes, disco biscuits and above all, disco records. A 12-incher was no longer a well-worn sexual innuendo, but an extended edition of a popular chart hit.

Of all the disco groups around, K.C. & the Sunshine Band must rate as one of the funkiest, grooviest and above all most financially successful. But many of their titles seem cryptic. As Dr. Fitzgerald explains:

❝ *They were obviously a band who were very much steeped in the songs and music of the 17th century. You see, that was when King Charles I was on the throne, after whom the lead singer K.C. was named, of course.*

'Shake Your Booty' for example, refers to the habit of parading one's spoils of war after battle. One would literally 'shake one's booty' in triumph. As for 'Get Down Tonight', well, that was a familiar cry in 17th century markets of street vendors selling duck feathers for warmth. 'Get Down Tonight!' they would cry. And of course, similarly with 'That's the Way I Like it'. Commonly misspelt it is, in fact, a declaration in praise of curdled milk: 'That's the Whey! I Like It'! I'm often asked how I account for the fact that they were all written in the mid-to-late 1970's when I claim they date back to the 1600's. But frankly I don't. I don't account for it at all. I ignore it entirely . . . Largely because it makes a complete nonsense of my argument. **❞**

Below *A middle of the road artist.*

---

[33]Not to be confused with Adult Orientated Rock a.k.a. Any Old Rubbish
[34]Their first achievement was to win the Eurovision Song Contest – not, in fact, much of an achievement; particularly since Israel could win it twice without even being in Europe.

But what was it like inside the clubs where disco was king? The place was alive with sexual friction. With the girls in their pencil skirts and high heels, standing in a circle near the dance-floor, you knew they were there for one thing – the dancing. And with the men in their T-shirts cut off at the shoulders, neatly pressed slacks and a comb in the left-hand back pocket, you knew they were there for one thing too – a rattling good shag.

The disco boom also affected the output of various groups who had started out as rock & rollers but began to tailor their music to the booming disco market. Pink Floyd, Led Zeppelin, and The Rolling Stones are not examples of such groups, but the Gibb Brothers most certainly are.

What can one say about the Bee Gees that hasn't already been said, and that isn't libellous? Compliments, praise for their lyrics, appreciation of their dress sense – there's quite a lot you could say about the Bee Gees that hasn't already been said, but what, in the end, would be the point? Suffice to say, they were the single most successful group of lyrically inept composers with no dress sense, to have come out of Australia since Rolf Harris.

The disco-movie of the decade was, of course, *Saturday Night Fever*, which featured the music of the Bee Gees and the acting and dancing of John Travolta. Despite this, the film became one of the biggest box office hits, and was also quite popular when it was shown in the cinema.

Travolta also starred in the other most successful pop-movie of all time, *Grease*, opposite Olivia Newton-John giving her now acclaimed screen debut as Sandy, a performance that became a prototype for method actors and for which she was inexplicably overlooked in the Oscar nominations for that year. It is now widely known that Marie Osmond turned down the part of Sandy before it was offered to Olivia, but something that's not such common knowledge is the fact that before Marie was approached, the part had been offered to a whole host of celebrities. Here are some of those who turned it down and the reasons they gave:

Linda Ronstadt
.... *'Recording'*
Tina Turner
.... *'In the studio'*
Donna Summer
.... *'In the studio'*
Andrei Sakharov
.... *'In internal exile'*
Dolly Parton
.... *'Visiting her sister Stella'*
Stella Parton
.... *'Visiting her sister Dolly'*
Ella Fitzgerald
.... *'Felt the part was too old'*
H.R.H. The Queen Mother
.... *'Not enough dosh'*
Zena Skinner
..... *'Part did not involve enough cooking'*
Jimmy Greaves
.... *'Must have the wrong number'*

Right *John Travolta pointing in the two directions his career has gone.*

71

SUPERSTARS – JUST HOW BIG WERE THEY?

The so-called Seventies was an era of superlatives, as solo artists vied to be bigger and better than their rivals. Names like Elton John, Rod Stewart, Donny Osmond . . . But who was the biggest?

Charlie Ronson:

" Very difficult to say. In terms of sheer enormity, you're looking at old stagers like Presley and some of the newer stars like Barry White. I really wouldn't like to guess who was the bigger. Presley, towards the end of his life was absolutely huge. I mean a total flab-bucket. But Barry White on the other hand was a real mountain of blubber. And how about Demis Roussos? Obscenely fat. And greasy with it. A disgusting avalanche of flesh. Moby Dick in a kaftan. And look at Manilow! O.K. maybe he's not so obese, but have you seen his nose? If that guy was on cocaine, he could snort the world's annual supply in one sniff. I mean, we are talking enormous here. You could dock a liner in one nostril. Come to think of it you gotta pretty huge snozzle yourself . . . "

(AT THIS POINT MR. RONSON REQUIRED A SEDATIVE)

ELTON JOHN

Someone who stood head and shoulders above other stars – but only when wearing his 36″ platform heels – was Elton John. In

Test pilot for Elton John's platform shoes.

the spring of 1977, Elton took his 'Philadelphia Freedom' to the people of Russia, receiving a particularly interesting review from the Russian newspaper *Pravda*.

В. И. ЛЕН

В Пол

Политбюро ЦК КПСС на очередном ELTON JOHN обсудило (REG. DWIGHT!) ные, политические и хозяйс WATFORD мероприятия, связанные с практической реа- FREEDOM решений июньского (1987 года) PHILADELPHIA ЦК КПСС. Утверждены организа- SPUTNIK MAN итические и пропа- DOSVEDANIA мероприятия, направленные на выполнение решений Пленума. Определены YELLOW BRICK ROAD рассмотрения замечаний и SONG FOR GUY, вы- BURGESS ых участниками Пленума ЦК КПСС. Одобрен разра- ботанный THE BITCH IS BACK стров СССР комплексный план осуществления практической перестройки MRS. THATCHER экономикой.

При ELTON JOHN и этих вопросов на заседании Политбюро NOT VERY GOOD HAIR TRANSPLANT к решению поставленных задач — в обеспечении реального ... широчайших народ- ...

дукци ция логиче нятые жаны трудя При полнит 1988 г емку н произв родно цию треб батыв мышл строй предпр матери издели нима котор крас преду ствен жил шко об

Someone who speaks Russian fluently is Prof. John Trevelli, lecturer in Soviet Studies at the University of Minnesota. Unfortunately however, we have not contacted him to translate this piece, as he lives in Minnesota.

ROD STEWART

The solo superstar who stood head and shoulders above Elton John (not difficult considering he's a midget) was the unmistakable 70s figures, tall, thin, blond, wearing impossibly tight trousers and rasping out songs in that distinctively gravelly voice. Not Bonnie Tyler, but the Tartan Terror, Rod Stewart – a working class Scottish lad, about whom the only thing that wasn't Scottish (apart from his accent, birthplace and parentage) was his conspicuous spending, as an old friend of his from Finsbury Park in North London, told us:

" I knew Rod when he was struggling to make ends meet. He often used to come round to my house and have a meal, and borrow some money. Then, of course, he started to get famous, but he never forgot us. He'd still come back now and again, and we'd have a meal together, a few drinks, and he'd borrow some money. Then he'd sleep with my wife and go off and tour America. After that, he became a superstar. And I'd still see him quite regularly. You know, on Top Of The Pops *or some TV special. But one thing I will say about old Rod. Success never changed him. Rich or poor, he was still a cocky, arrogant, tight-fisted little bastard. "*

At the end of the 1970s Rod became one of the brave band of English pioneers like

Rod Stewart enjoys a dribble with David Steele.

Mick Jagger (and later Frankie Goes To Hollywood) who left England to spread the message of rock round the world, to spread excitement wherever they went – but, above all, to spread their earnings to avoid paying income tax in their own country.

In America he became more famous for his sexual antics than his records, going out with a succession of models who proved Einstein's second theory of relativity (that length of a leg is inverse proportion to the quantity of grey matter up top).

But age has started to take its toll of him and people have started to ask – does he still enjoy sex, or does he now just lie back and think of Ekland?

GILBERT O'SULLIVAN

Not all the giant superstars of the 70s were millionaires. One notable case was an Irishman in a cloth cap who took his stage name from the famous W.S. Gilbert and Arthur Sullivan. But W.S. Arthur was not

W.S. Arthur.

to enjoy any major success, and so he changed his name to Gilbert O'Sullivan. This proved to be the key to success but he was to see almost no money until he sued his manager some 10 years later. We paid a visit to this so-called manager, whom we shall call Mr. K. (the K standing for Kirkpatrick, his real name) to see if there was any truth behind the allegations of his mercenary conduct. He said 'there is absolutely no truth in it whatsoever', and charged us £50 to print it.

KATE BUSH

Of all the lovely girls of the Seventies, few made a greater impact than Kate Bush who was only 16 when she was discovered by Dave Gilmour of Pink Floyd who was immensely impressed by her musical ability, her precocity, and the way in which she kept falling out of her leotard. Kate spent the next two years in intensive study of dance and mime. She became a good dancer and a superb mime artist. Unfortunately, however, she still insisted on singing in a strangled high pitched whine. Despite her records though, Kate Bush became a big star, mainly because as her vocal range got larger, her leotards got smaller. She hit a quiet note in the early eighties but in 1985 she was back hitting lots of noisy notes and scored a big success with a collection of her greatest hits entitled 'Complete Madness'.[35]

[35] Authors' mistake. This was the title of a compilation by Madness. The title of Kate Bush's album was of course 'Complete Insanity'.

Right *Sid Vicious (Please check before printing).*

The King Is Dead

Who can forget that tragic day when the news flashed around the world that the man they called 'The King' was dead . . .

```
87-07-20   12:01
*
263879 NATMAG G
7973   87-07-20   10:52
-----------------------------------------

THE KING IS DEAD.  BUCKINGHAM PALACE HAS ANNOUNCED
THAT GEORGE VI DIED PEACEFULLY IN HIS SLEEP THIS
MORNING.  A NATION MOURNS.
```

And only a few years later came even more tragic news . . .

```
EVEN MORE TRAGIC NEWS.  THE KING IS STILL ALIVE.
IT WAS ANNOUNCED TODAY THAT JONATHAN KING
IS STILL ALIVE.  A NATION MOURNS.
```

Then in 1977 came the most tragic news of all:

```
THE MOST TRAGIC NEWS OF ALL.  SHARE PRICES HAVE
HIT AN ALL-TIME LOW EXCLAMATION MARK.  PANIC ON
WALL STREET EXCLAMATION MARK STOCK EXCHANGE IN
CHAOS.  THE POUND TUMBLES.  MORE FOLLOWS...

ALVIN PRESLEY, A POP SINGER
DIED THIS MORNING AT HIS MEMPH
```

Elvis Presley, the man they called 'The King Of Rock & Roll' died at 3.30 p.m. on 16th August, 1977. Around the world radio and television programmes were interrupted to report the tragedy. Within minutes, thousands of distraught people phoned radio and televison companies to complain about the loss of their favourite programmes.

His faithful fans, however, refuse to believe that The King is dead, citing a confusion registered on his death certificate. Elvis's biographer, Tom Cross, clears up the mystery:

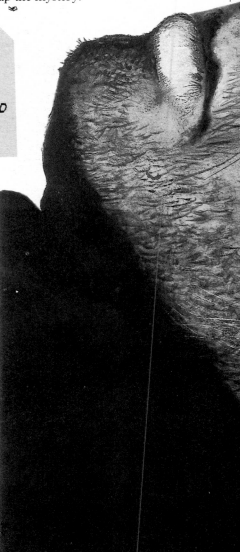

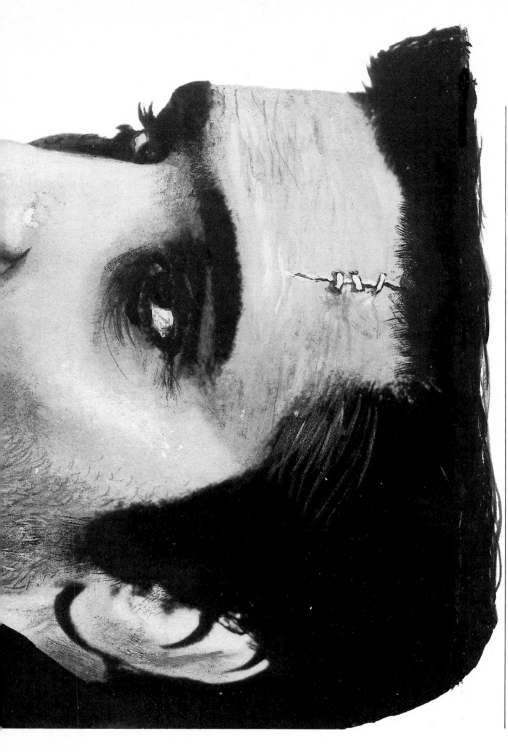

> ❝ *The confusion occurs because there is a difference between Presley's clinical death and brain death.*
>
> *'Clinical death' occurs when the heart stops beating and I have established beyond doubt that that occurred at precisely 3.30 on the afternoon of 16th August, 1977.*
>
> *On the other hand, Presley's 'brain death' occurred in 1959.* ❞

With Elvis's death an era was ended but his memory lives on and today he's commemorated in The Rock & Roll Hall Of Fame where he has a room to himself as he is far too fat to share it with anyone else.[31]

Others to be found in The Rock & Roll Hall Of Fame are those fragile flowers who were tragically plucked too early including such casualties of The Seventies as Jim Morrison, Jimi Hendrix and Keith Moon. Mama Cass Elliott – who started out in a little Greenwich village coffee house, moved on to a Pizza Parlour by Central Park and ended up in a Macdonalds on 52nd St, before having lunch – also has a large room to herself.

These and the rest of the tragic bouquet of plucked flowers had consumed life with the same enthusiasm that they had consumed vast quantities of drugs and alcohol. They lived life in the fast lane, but they'd think that preferable to living life in the bus lane and getting run down by a number 88 from Dollis Hill.

Sic Transit Gloria Gaynor.

[31] It can be found by walking down Rock & Roll The Hall of Fame, turning right into the Rock & Roll Corridor of Fame, past The Rock & Roll Dining Room of Fame and asking again by The Roll & Roll Toilet of Fame.

Left *Living in a box... Elvis Presley, 1977.*

THE GOBFATHERS

1977 was the Year of the Punks. The year in which music became tasteless, vile and repulsive: David Soul, Terry Wogan, Boney M. But there was also a new style of music. At long last the pretentiousness of the mid-70s was smashed by the upsurge of punk in Britain and from the States, New Wave.

Some claim that New Wave came first, others maintain that punk started before that, and most couldn't give a monkey's. Indeed, like the Monkees, many of the punk bands didn't actually play on their first singles. Not because they weren't up to it, but because they were too good. Instead, they would use not session musicians, but members of the public whom they would drag in off the street.

But one of the most puzzling aspects of punk was why so many of the bands, the Sex Pistols, the Buzzcocks, the Hot Rods, the Members and the Tubes, to name but several, all called themselves by sexual innuendos referring to male private parts. Such a savage, anti-establishment stand had not been seen since the days of the 'Carry On' films.

Of the punk and New Wave bands around, the most extreme was one which went under the comparatively unsubtle name of The Penises. For a start, whereas most bands smashed up their equipment after the show, they smashed it up before the show. They were so anarchic, they wouldn't perform at all. And while the other punks may have put pins and chains through their ears and noses, the Penises used to drive safety pins into their temples and arteries. So unconventional were they, in fact, that they would regularly kill themselves.[36]

THoSE SEX PISTOls

The Sex Pistols were formed by Malcolm McLaren, for many the founding Father of Punk, who hit upon the brilliantly simple idea of putting together the four most obnoxious men he could find and persuading the media that they were the new face of rock. The whole band set out to shock and offend. Johnny Rotten would stub lighted cigarettes out on his arm, slash his flesh with razors and was even known to sneeze without using a hanky. But could anything be more abhorrent than his most offensive personal habit – his insistence on opening his mouth as wide as possible and using it to sing? But how did McLaren make the Sex Pistols such a phenomenal success? An extract from his appointment diary shows how it was achieved:

August

Tuesday 14

10am. Press Conference. Announce split up of band

11am. Arrange drug arrest in hotel room for Sid

11.30am. Press Conference. Announce reformation of band.

2.30pm. Offend T.V. presenter on-air

4.30pm. Arrange unexpected bout of violence between band backstage

5.00pm. Press Conference. Announce split up of band.

6.00pm. Announce last minute cancellation of Concert.

6.30pm. Press Conference. Announce split up of band – appologise for having called them in twice

9.00pm. Organise Drug O/D.

9.30pm. Call Ambulance to take Johnny to nearest hospital, following shock O/D.

11.00pm Cocoa, brush teeth, say prayers and kiss Teddy.

78

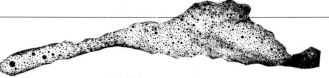

Malcolm McLaren was to go on to become the master manipulator of the media and of underage girls he met in laundrettes. He was to travel the world and absorb a vast amount of musical styles and subsequently absorb a vast amount of royalties from ripping off unsuspecting amateur musicians.

The Sex Pistols came to national attention when they appeared in a now notorious television interview with Bill Grundy. Thousands of viewers phoned in to complain about the loutish, drunken conduct, the uncouth, dishevelled clothing and the obscene language. And several also complained about the Sex Pistols.

As a result of that interview, the Pistols were signed to EMI. But within a few days, they had dropped them. Mr. Robert Todd, then a director of the company recalls the events of those days vividly, and remembers why:

❝ *I have an excellent memory.* **❞**

He also remembers what happened during those days.

❝ *Well, shortly after the Sex Pistols had left the building one day, we discovered that the chairman's gold pen had been stolen. We noticed his desk had also been ransacked, and someone had urinated over the carpet. It then came to our attention that his executive rubber plant had been set on fire and words had been*

---

36 Another youth movement of the time was The Pinks who were less extreme Preferring Blue Tack and depilatory cream to pins and razors.

Right *Kate Bush.*

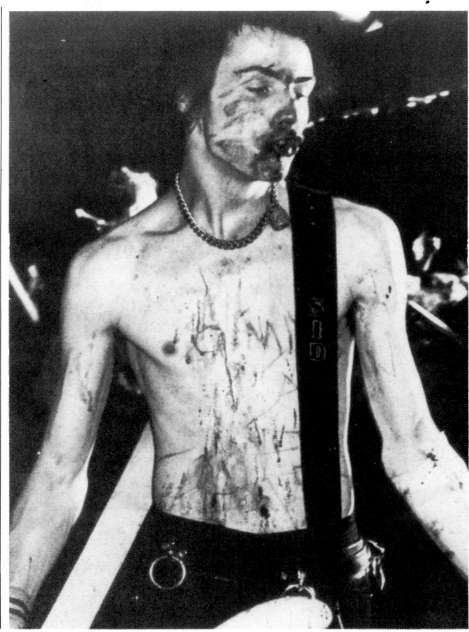

79

The infamous tupperware party at the Chelsea Hotel.

Sid & Nancy in the Midland Region finals of 'Come Dancing' (or as it became known 'Scum Dancing').

scrawled over his walls. In blood. In fact, in the chairman's own blood. Whom we then noticed was hanging upside down from the light-fitting. And so the chairman – the new chairman, that is – decided to do without the services of the Sex Pistols. But we made it quite clear that we parted company on the most amicable of terms. "

The punks felt they were a threat to the organised structure of society, a society that filled them with contempt and anger. And though their music lacked the finesse and precision of what had gone before, at least punk songs had something to say – even though you couldn't for the life of you make out what the hell it was.

Perhaps the philosophy of punk rock was summed up by one of the foremost bands of the time, for many the Uncles of Punk, the Stranglers.[37] Their message was: 'Never believe anyone who's over 30'. And the fact that most of the band were well over 30 when they said that, seems to be the proof of it.

Someone who was for many the 'Not a Proper Uncle But A Close Friend Of The Family Of Punk' was Paul Weller of The Jam. His great claim to fame is that, unlike other former punks, he has NEVER sold out. There were always plenty of seats left at his concerts.

Most certainly the 'Not A Proper Aunt But Someone Who Comes Round When Mummy's Not In' was Patti Smith. Her concerts were often unusual in so far as they began with an hour long poetry recital, whether the audience liked it or not. She claimed that she often wrote poetry whilst masturbating, which is perhaps why many eminent professors of literature have come to refer to it as 'a bit of a wank'.

[37]Not to be confused with Bill Haley the Uncle of Rock or Charles Haley – the uncle of Bill.

Left *Lead singer of the Penises, one of four members.*
Right *Bill Grundy after disagreeing with the Sex Pistols.*

THE EIGHTIES:
THE 'NOT OVER YET' DECADE

The whirligig of time spins on, as we come to rest at the start of a new era, a new decade and most importantly a new chapter. The Eighties was above all the decade of innovation and novelty. Things were changing on the music scene, and changing fast.

The very first No. 1 record of the decade, for example, was by a little known group called Pink Floyd, and a year later it was the turn of Joe 'Shaddap You Face' Dolce – a new star for a new decade who came from nowhere, scored a Number One hit and then, mercifully, returned to nowhere–or, to be precise, Belgium. And in between, the world was treated to a new Christmas hit for a new decade – 'There's No-one Quite Like Grandma' by St. Winifred's School Choir[38] – one of the earliest adverts for the advantages of condoms.[39]

TECHNO-ROCK

With the 80's came a completely new sound – the sound of technology. Yes, the micro-chip and computer had at last come to rock.

Gary Numan's first hit, 'Are Trains Electric?' was the first to be written on a digital watch, played on a pocket calculator, and sung by a Speak Your Weight machine with bleached, thinning hair. And what record could have been more

[38] A tribute to Tina Turner
[39] Too late, unfortunately to influence the parents of The Jacksons, The Osmonds and Five Star.

Left *Gary Numan – a man, a mission, a twat.*

appropriate for a new decade? Well, almost any, but nonetheless Gary Numan had two Number One hits, largely due to his startling performing style which was described as having all the verve, energy and excitement of tarmac. Perhaps this explains why he won the ultimate accolade of being the only living pop star on permanent exhibition at Madam Tussaud's who calculated that they saved £2,000 in wax.[40]

Below *Firewerk.*

Techno-rock was music in which instruments were replaced by synthesizers and drum machines, musicians by computer programmers, and singers by small black boxes with winking lights, that could be programmed to do anything a rock star could do. Well, almost anything. No machine yet invented could perform the most important functions of the rock star: snorting cocaine, catching clap off a groupie and smashing up hotel rooms.[41]

The aim of techno-rock was to reduce

music to its very simplest element with the aid of thousands of pounds of highly sophisticated electronic equipment. And so established have the German band Kreftwerk become that they can now be studied on school syllabuses along with Fretwerk and Needlewerk. But what has

[40]The wax saved was subsequently used on the model of Meatloaf as his earlobe.

[41] However, a sign of the changing times is the fact that one group, The Beauty Boys, have been banned from The Holiday Inn chain for redecorating their rooms in Sandersen wallpaper and Laura Ashley fabrics.

the overall effect of techno-rock been on the music scene? Dr.Fitzgerald:

" *If I said we're talking hands-on experience with fifth-generation, state-of-the-art synthesizer hardware interfaced with user-friendly,* info-retrievable peripherals with which you can download either modems or mainframes, I don't expect you'd know what I was talking about. But then, that wouldn't surprise me, because I'm buggered if I do either. "

NEW ROMANTICS

The most important innovation of the Eighties was the wealth of new bands who made their impact on the scene. And the earliest flowering of an Eighties' style was the group of strutting young peacocks who called themselves the New Romantics. But sadly it was also the decade of the Old Romantics. In fact, the Geriatric Romantics:

The birth of the New Romantics took place in basement clubs in London where groups like Ultravox, Spandau Ballet and Blue Rondo à la Turk first gathered to dance to their own brand of music, dress up in outrageous clothes, show off their latest make-up and spend hours deciding whether to use the ladies' or gentlemen's toilets.

The most important club of the time was Blitz run by Steve Strange. And the second most important was Dachau run by Steve Slightly-Unusual, who has fond memories of those days:

Above *Julio Yglesias, one of the new rheumatics.*

" *A lot of the New Romantics were formed down my club. A few of the boys would get together and start a group. But most of them didn't last long and they split up due to artistic policy. Mostly it was because their clothes clashed. And you'd always get one bloke who insisted on wearing diamante when the rest of* the band were really into feathers. So they were always falling out. And then they'd make up. Or sometimes they'd do their make-up first, and then fall out. "

The essence of the New Romantics was style. The clothes, the make-up, the image were all-important. So anyone could become a star in the early Eighties, as long as they had long, flowing hair, wore layers and layers of mascara, and dressed in glamorous party frocks. Anyone, that is, except women. Faced with this problem, many female singers started dressing like men.

Annie Lennox of the Eurythmics took cross-dressing so far that in one video she played a woman pretending to be a man pretending to be a woman. Or possibly a man pretending to be a woman pretending to be a man. Amidst all this gender-bending some people gave up their sexual identity altogether and simply settled for looking like Michael Jackson. Not easy because Michael Jackson spent millions of dollars on plastic surgery trying to look like anybody but Michael Jackson.

THE BEATLES OF THE 80'S

DURAN DURAN

The band that must surely have come closest to being The Beatles of Their Day, since, like the Beatles, they were a blond five-some from Leighton Buzzard, was Duran Duran. Their image of being a teeny-bopper group whose fans were all under 10,

was not helped by the appointment of Amanda Stubbs as the president of their fan club.

Despite the fact that the majority of 'Durannies' were barely potty-trained, the group had a massive rise to stardom, and their announcement in 1985 to disband rocked the rock world.

Duran Duran split into two groups, Duran and Duran. They then decided to call Arcadia, and the other after a municipal building in Battersea, the Dog's Home, which described their music.

HUMAN LEAGUE

The group who perhaps more than any, deserved the title of 'The Beatles of Their Day', consisting, as they did, of a lead singer with half a head of hair and two token bits of totty, was Human League.

Their pioneering style of twin lead harmonic vocals, syncopated baseline rhythm sections, and singing flat, really caught on, and it wasn't long before the idea was taken to its extreme by Soft Cell.

SPANDAU BALLET

Here was a group of New Romantics that took its name from the grim German prison where the notorious Nazi, Rudolph Hess, was jailed, and by amusingly juxtaposing that with the word 'ballet', created an intriguing and yet totally meaningless title.

But despite their name they were still going strong in the late Eighties. They have come 'Through the Barricades' without a hair out of place and people have managed to answer Tony Hadley's heartfelt question in *True*: 'Why do I find it hard to write the next line?' – because

you don't write the lyrics of the songs, you great wassock!

CULTURE CLUB

The real stars of the Eighties, and the band that most experts on the subject tend to regard as the modern-day 'Beatles of their era', was Culture Club – the super-group that came to the fore in 1982, lead by one George O'Dowd, a man who, in the eyes of Charlie Ronson is no ordinary man:

"*In my opinion, which in my opinion is truth in its most absolute form, Boy George was quite plainly a woman. And what makes it doubly obscene is the he used to wear his hair in long ringlets, sported a Hassidic chapeau, used to apply enough face powder to choke Manhattan, was extremely overweight, and had male genitalia. In short, the sort of woman I despise.***"**

Nevertheless, Boy George's appeal to both men and women alike was and indeed is enormous. True, he had not been a success in Greece where he was stoned on stage, but that was for the simple reason that, after Demis Roussos, the Greeks had had quite enough of listening to fat men in dresses.

What was the secret behind the Culture Club sound? Many have likened George's voice to that of Smokey Robinson. But Dr. Fitzgerald prefers to go slightly further back in time:

" *No doubt about it. The person, Boy George has to thank for his rise to super-stardom is Boadicea. Firstly because she wore a great deal of face powder, far too much make-up and a frock, and lastly because if she hadn't have been around, Caesar wouldn't have bothered to invade Britain. Now, if Caesar hadn't conquered Britain and brought civilisation to this country, we'd have had no government and therefore no William Pitt. He it was whose legislation led to the slave trade which brought so many Africans to the shores of America, of which of course Muddy Waters is one. Now, Muddy Waters it was who paved the way for soul singers of the 60s such as Smokey Robinson, whose blend of soul and gospel strongly influenced Boy George and was the secret behind Culture Club's success.* **"**

Boy George's career hit a rapid personal and financial decline after the release of the flop album 'Waking Up and Finding I Hadn't Got Any Trousers On' – but 1987 saw him back at the top of the charts again with the song 'Everything I Own (I've Spent On Heroin)'.

FRANKIE GOES TO HOLLYWOOD

Perhaps the greatest success story of the 1980s, and in that way mirroring most closely the success of The Beatles, was that of Frankie Goes To Hollywood. Their first single happened to catch the attention of

Boy George. A man who preferred a cup of tea to sex.

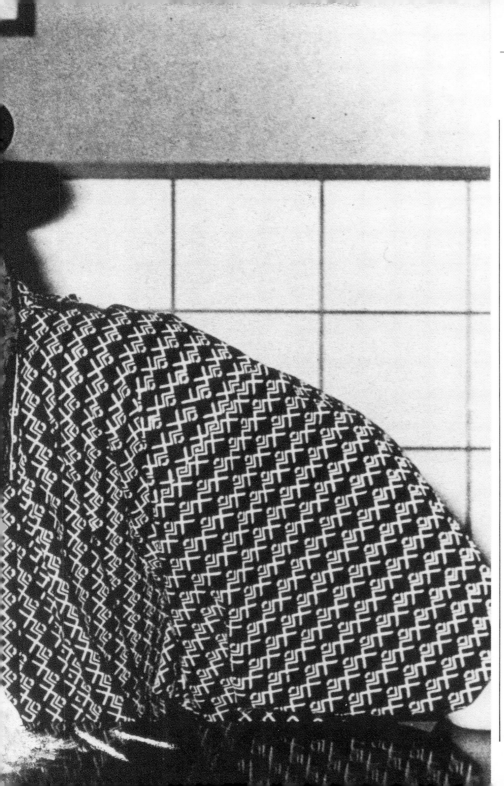

the most powerful man in British rock. Just one word for him and obscure records would race to number one. The man with this awesome power was disc jockey Mike Read who looked like Cliff Richard and thought he was the reincarnation of Sir John Betjeman. Mike needed to hear the record no more than 54 times before deciding it was unfit to be played on his radio programme. The B.B.C. instantly banned the record which immediately shot to the top of the charts and, not surprisingly, the Radio 1 switchboard was jammed the next day by people ringing in to protest that Mike Read hadn't banned their records.

'Relax' went on to become the biggest-selling single of the 80s in and its re-mixed versions – 7″, 12″, 15″ and 19″ VIP model – and they remain the only group in history to issue a Greatest Hits LP on which all 12 tracks are the same song. And as if that wasn't enough, the records were out-sold by 'Relax' t-shirts, which Mike Read also refused to play.

Ever since their first hit, lead singer Holly Johnson has been making the headlines, and never more so than around the time of the 1985 BPI Awards when he announced in front of a live television audience that he had never actually met Prince, but he'd had sex with him on the telephone. Thankfully the producers were able to cut to a commercial break, before Holly added that it was the most pleasurable reverse charge he'd ever experienced.

Frankie became notorious for their wild antics – smashing up hotels, dressing rooms and even their instruments, although this last bit of destruction didn't **89** count for much since they didn't play them anyway. On the occasion when they smashed up the stage in the Montreux Festival, however, they were quite careful to get permission in advance . . .

Dear Sir,
This is to confirm the schedule for Sunday: 6pm sound check; 7 pm on stage; 7.05 'Relax', 'Power of Love' & 'Welcome to the Pleasure Dome'; 7.35 demolish set; 8 o'clock backstage Press Conference; 8.30 leave for hotel.
Yours sincerely . . . Holly Johnson

Dear Mr. Johnson,
Thank you for your letter regarding the running-order for Sunday. Could I please draw your attention to the 7.35 pm entry 'demolish set'. Is this a misprint or is it your intention to destroy the stage?
Yours sincerely . . . Gerhardt Zuppinger

Dear Mr. Zuppinger,
Just to confirm that we shall be destroying instruments, amplifiers, scenery and stage area. Hope this ties in with your plans.
Yours . . . Holly

Dear Mr. Holly,
I think you may be labouring under the misapprehension that the demolition of our stage here at Montreux is an everyday occurrence. I'm afraid this will not be possible.
Yours sincerely . . . Gerhardt Zuppinger

Dear Gerhardt,
How about £5,000. Love . . . Holly

Dear Holly,
Done! . . . Love Gerhardt[42]

PAUL HARDCASTLE

One of the stars of the 80s who could so easily have been a star of the 60s, and in that way has nothing in common with the Beatles, was Paul Hardcastle. He it was who took a lot of 1960s documentary footage of the Vietnam war and intercut it with bits of music that he hoped nobody would notice sounded just like Mike Oldfield's 'Tubular Bells'. Unfortunately for him, one of the people who did notice was Mike Oldfield who ended up getting a co-writing credit for the record. And shortly afterwards he also gave a writing credit to the North Vietnamese and American governments for making the whole song possible.

The song was entitled, 'N-N-N-Nineteen' and referred to the average age of American soldiers in Vietnam, and not, as many thought, to the average IQ of Bananarama. Paul's next record was the aptly named 'Just for the Money'. Just as 'N-N-N-Nineteen' had dealt with the up-to-the-minute issue of the Vietnam war, 'Just for the Money' tackled the contemporary issue that was on everyone's lips: the N-N-N-Nineteen Sixty-Three Great Train

[42]Subsequently, Frankie found smashing their instruments too tiring so they hired session musicians to do it for them.

Frankie says "welcome to the scrap heap".

Robbery. Following its only limited success and quite spectacular failure, plans were scrapped for his next record, which was to have concerned the most burning question for modern day youth: Was Anthony Eden right to invade the Suez Canal in N-N-N-Nineteen Fifty Six? Instead, Paul turned his attention to 'F-F-F-Fifty Three', a record dealing with the average age of the Rolling Stones.

MADONNA

One of the biggest names ever to emerge from the States is Madonna Louise Ciccone. Little wonder, therefore, that she reduced it to simply Madonna. It is ironic that the woman who was without doubt the sex symbol of the Eighties (someone who's done more for the secondhand clothes shops than Oxfam) should be named after the Virgin Mary, especially considering she is neither called Mary, nor a particularly religious person. Clearly, there is more to Madonna that meets the groin, but how did it all start?

Sam 'Friend To All The Stars' Chuck reveals:

" *I remember when Madonna came to me one day as I was polishing my medallion collection and she said, 'Mr. Chuck, I want to become an instant rock & roll legend.' I said, 'Can you sing?' and she said, 'No'. So I said, 'You got good legs?' And she said, 'No, Mr. Chuck, they're like tree trunks.' So I said, 'What you need is a gimmick. Go and get yourself a navel.' And she said, 'Mr. Chuck,*

Right *Madonna – the material girl whose material didn't reach her navel.*

I have one of them already.' And I said, 'You got it on you?' And she said, 'Yup,' and I said, 'Well, lift up your shirt and show it on TV and you'll become an instant rock & roll legend.' And she said, 'I'll do that, Mr. Chuck,' and that's how she became an instant rock & roll legend. **99**

Since becoming an instant rock & roll legend, Madonna has certainly lived up to her name, by acting like a real prima donna. At the American Live Aid concert, for example, her bodyguards were ordered to clear everybody, including the other stars and organisers, from the backstage area, so that she could use the toilet in privacy. They were only prevented from clearing the stadium of 40,000 people, when it was explained to them that she could do it herself in half the time, just by singing.

Her marriage to Sean Penn was kept a strictly private affair to which only the bride's 5000 closest friends were invited. Security was also kept so tight that only 10,000 members of the press were allowed to witness the ceremony. Nevertheless her bodyguards sorted out the ensuing chaos and followed their orders to the letter in keeping everyone away from the bride. Sadly, they did it so successfully that it was a fortnight before the marriage was consummated.

Her film career has seen her acting opposite her husband in *Shanghai Surprise* – and the sexual electricity between Penn and Madonna has not been seen on screen since the heyday of Abbot and Costello.

Right *Prince looking for the ladder in order to talk to his minder.*

PRINCE

Another big name to come out of the States in the early Eighties was Prince. Many in Britain will remember his truly unforgettable acceptance of the 1985 B.P.I. Award, combining as it did the longest ever walk with the shortest ever speech to produce one of the year's most memorable passages of sheer tedium. Nevertheless, that night he became one of the first rock stars to use the trendy status symbol of the decade – a minder. Ever since, every rock star has had to have their own minder, preferably a very large, very aggressive, heavily-muscled bodyguard who would make Rambo look like Marc Almond. And who would make Marc Almond look like tomato purée if he was stupid enough to get in the way.

In the mid-Eighties Prince went into temporary retirement announcing that he had 'gone to look for the ladder'. Some interpreted this as meaning he was looking for spiritual enlightenment, a view very much *not* shared by Dr. Fitzerald:

66 *I think when he said he was looking for a ladder, he meant he was looking for a ladder. You see, Prince is remarkably small, one of the most truly small rock stars around in fact, and obviously he's got fed up not being able to see what everybody else is getting up to. So he said to himself, 'Now, what ho Prince!' he's said, 'Go out and get yourself a nice sturdy ladder, and you jolly well scoot up it and see what it is that everybody's been getting up to.* **99**

This is not a theory which is upheld by anything that Prince himself has ever said, however. When asked for an explanation of 'the ladder' he is quoted as saying, 'Sometimes it snows in April. The wind blows, a dog barks and the caravan moves on.' And when asked for an explanation of that, he added, 'The cucumber will lie down with the walrus.'

Dr. Fitzgerald has an equally forthright interpretation of this:

" *He's obviously lost his marbles.* **"**

Prince has lived out his secret fantasies in his films. In *Purple Rain* his obsession with the colour purple and dressing up in purple clothes shows that fundamentally he would rather like to be a bishop, while *Under the Cherry Moon* has shown that fundamentally he is a very bad film maker.

WHAM!

Mention the names of songs such as 'Careless Whisper', 'Freedom', 'Wake Me Up Before You Go Go', and 'Wham! Rap' to anyone over the age of 6, and one word will spring to their lips – WHAM! Unless they're Belgian, of course, in which they'd probably say Hawkwind or Uriah Heep. But that's not to take anything away from the achievements of the explosive duo, who were rarely out of our newspapers. Indeed at one time they were rarely out of the law courts and Barry Manilow claimed that 'Last Christmas' was taken from one of his hits 'Can't Smile Without You'. Another wrangle followed after the realisation that 'Freedom' and 'I'm Your Man' were so similar that they would have to sue themselves for plagiarism.

Before their historic split, interest in George Michael and Andrew Ridgeley's private life (or public life as it's called when you're a rock star) was insatiable. Nor was it restricted to Britain, as is shown by this clipping from the French journal *France-Soir*.

Les Garçons De Wham!!

Hier soir, George Michael et Andrew Ridgeley allaient danser dans un nightclub a Londres qui s'appelle Hommes-de-Ficelle. Quand ils sortaient, ils engageaient dans un massacre de photographes, pendant lequel un journaliste recevait un genou dans les testicules. En tombant, il a crié que M. Ridgeley était 'un wanker complet', et il a décrit leur nouveau disque comme un grand tas de merde. M. Michael venait lui aider, mais recevait aussi un coup dans les goolies. Le photographe poursuit maintenant Andrew Ridgeley pour avoir ruiné son abilité de faire le jig-jig.

TRANSLATION READS:
Yesterday evening, George Michael and Andrew Ridgeley went dancing in a London nightclub called Stringfellows. As they were leaving, they were involved in a slight skirmish with photographers, in which one journalist received a blow to the groin. As he fell, he called Mr. Ridgeley a 'silly chap', and described their latest record as a below-par recording. Mr. Michael came to his aid but also received an abdominal injury. The photographer is now suing Andrew Ridgeley for having ruined his married life.

In 1985 Wham! were the first group to visit China where they made a tremendous impact although they caused some puzzlement. The programme for their concert translated the title of 'Careless Whisper' as 'Speaking Frankly Without Evil Intent' and 'Freedom' became 'We Have Had To Apply For Relief From The Government'. However, the Chinese were completely unable to interpret 'Wake Me Up Before You Go–Go'. Hardly surprising, since we're still waiting for it to be translated into English.

The Wham! split in 1986 is now legend. But for years many people had seen it coming. Despite the popularity of the two-some, it was frankly only a matter of time before Andrew Ridgeley decided to go solo. After all, to be brutally honest, all George Michael did was write and sing the songs, whilst Andrew Ridgeley single-handedly had to take care of ALL the tambourine waving and ALL the handclapping. How could Andrew afford to support his old school chum any longer?[43]

---

[43]Since when George Michael has revelled in his solo status by making duets with Elton John and Aretha Franklin. However, his 1987 hit 'I Want Your Sex' was banned by radio and TV stations in Britain. As The Head of Banning Records at the B.B.C. explained, 'After listening carefully to the record, we decided that the lyrics are deeply offensive. But not as blatantly offensive as the music.'

The Chinese top ten at the time of Wham's visit.

HIT PALADE

		Last Week
1	**THE HERDSMEN OF THE PRAIRIE LOVE YOU, CHAIRMAN HUA** The People's Song Writing Collective PALRAPHONE	1
2	**SONG OF THE HYDRAULIC DAM PROJECT** The People's Song Writing Collective CHLYSALIS	2
3	**MARCH ON BRAVE WORKERS OF THE PADDY FIELDS** The People's Song Writing Collective WALNEL BLOS.	3
4	**WAKE ME UP BEFORE YOU GO-GO** Wham RONDON	197
5	**LITTLE RED BOOK** The People's Song Writing Collective PORYGRAM	5
6	**LITTLE RED BOOK AMENDMENTS** The People's Song Writing Collective EREKTRA	6
7	**GO AWAY YOU CAPITALIST RUNNING DOGS** The People's Song Writing Collective ATRANTIC	7
8	**WE CAN WORK IT OUT, WITH THE HELP OF THE MEMBERS OF THE COMMUNE** The People's Song Writing Collective CORUMBIA	8
9	**EMBROIDERING FOR CHAIRMAN HUA, CHAIRMAN MAO AND THE CHAIRMAN OF THE STANDING COMMITTEE OF THE NATIONAL PEOPLE'S CONGRESS** The People's Song Writing Collective PORYDOL	–
10	**LET'S ALL INCREASE THE AGRICULTURAL OUTPUT OF THE CHUNG KING REGION** The People's Song Writing Collective CHALISMA	10

15 Asked to sing theme for new James Bond film. Move on 1

16 Turn it down. Move on 12.

17 You are chosen as the new presenter of *The Tube*. Advance one.

18 You discover you're co-presenting it with Leslie Ash. Move back nine.

19 Meet Nick Kamen. Move on the number of his IQ times the throw of the dice. (i.e. If you throw 6, 6 x –1 = –6, so move back 6.)

14 Nominated Most Promising Newcomer at BPI Awards. Back 3.

13 And produced by Barry Gibb. Back 10.

12 New single is engineered by Trevor Horn. Move on 1 space.

11 Discover charts in question are Belgian Top 150. Back 1.

>>>GO

HOW TO BE A STAR

1 You are Andrew Ridgeley. Return to Go.

2 You win the chance to meet Gary Davies. Miss a turn.

3 You avoid the chance to meet Janice Long. Advance one.

4 Someone suggests forming a band. Throw again.

5 Your band secures first live-date at famous London night-spot. Move on a space.

20 Your 2nd album charts in America. Move on

21 Means you have to go and live there. Waste two years of your life, so miss a turn.

22 Record a duet with Sheena Easton. Move back 5.

23 Record company decide not to release it. Move on 5.

10 You're informed first album has entered charts. Move on 1.

9 First album receives rave notices from NME. Move back 3.

8 Talent scout is Jonathan King. Move back 5.

7 Spotted by a talent scout. Move on 1.

6 Turns out to be Victoria Station. Move back 3.

27 Move back to Britain. Miss a go and allow time to adapt to the climate.

28 Third album is chosen as Radio 2's "Record of the Week". Move back 10.

29 Invited to appear on this year's Royal Variety Performance. Move on 1.

26 Debbie Harry comes and stands next to you. Don't move anywhere.

30 Accept. Move back 30. Career over.

31 Decide to pack it in. Just do the odd cabaret here and there in smaller venues. Back to square one.

25 Spring - steen claims on TV he thought you were the backing singer and has never heard of you. Move back to 24

32 Die from drug overdose/ alcoholism/ plane crash. At last you're a star!

24 Record a duet with Bruce Springsteen. Move on to 25.

CHAPTER 16

LIVE AID THE SPIRIT OF '86*

The most heartening trend of 1986 was for rock stars to get together to record singles or perform concerts for charity. The record which started it all was of course Band Aid, but one group of people were largely unmoved by the general air of goodwill. A group of unrepresentative and largely unpopular people known as the British Government. Initially they stated that they were 'fully behind this organisation which has the power to raise such enormous amounts of money and affect everybody's life, and which is doing such a marvellous job'. Sadly, however, they were referring to the Inland Revenue, and so the tax on the Band Aid single was never removed.

But what of the event itself? What was its effect on people? A look at some of the letters to *The Times* the next day shows some of the different reactions:

Sir,
Yesterday's Live Aid concert was a triumph, a marvellous project in every respect. I watched it at my hockey club and we all agreed it was a tremendous achievement to get all those groups to give their services for free. I can't praise them highly enough.

Yours,
Nigel Rawlinson, Tunbridge Wells.

P.S. What were those pictures of starving children all about?

---

*The Authors would like it known that they are fully aware of the fact that Live Aid in fact took place in 1985, but having chosen to call the piece 'The Spirit of '86' to evoke memories of the spirit of '66, they felt it would only be confusing to them refer to it as having taken place when it did in 1985.

Sir,

What an obscene waste of time and youthful energy this so-called 'Live Aid' concert was. How anyone can use the word 'concert' to describe the playing of such music, I do not know, and frankly, if children today spent a little less time going to pop concerts and did a bit of National Service, then instead of just frittering away their youth giving money to people on the other side of the world, they could kill them. And they'd get a decent hair-cut out of it as well.

Yours,
Dorothy Kinsman, Berkshire.

Sir,

Being a man of the cloth, I was particularly uplifted by the marvellous efforts of all those involved in the Live Aid project, and was just about to dig deep into my pocket to send my donation in to the appropriate address, when this nasty Irishman suddenly came on the screen and started swearing at me. I'm afraid it completely put me off.

Yours,
Rev. John Pigeon, Little Thodding, Bucks.

Band Aid paved the way for many other charity singles, and a year later scores of pop stars and media celebrities gathered together for the benefit of one group of people who had been overlooked – they were penniless, ragged, painfully under-nourished, and had no work. And so the entire proceeds of the single went directly to the members of the Boomtown Rats.

At the now almost worthwhile B.P.I.

Left *Prince collects his award at the 1985 BPI ceremony.*

Awards, after Paul Young had picked up the Best Male Singer Award for his out-standing performance on every single groove of the one record he had released that year, Bob Geldof received a special award for the Band Aid single. His speech caused a furore when he claimed the situa-tion was worse than the concentration camps of Nazi Germany. Unfortunately, those listening were not aware that he was not referring to the Ethiopian famine, but to the Awards Ceremony itself.

The 1980's have in fact seen a prolifera-tion of these annual back-slapping cere-monies.★ It seemed reasonable when B.B.C. and I.T.V. started presenting their Music Awards, but then every local radio station, and every rock journal soon fol-lowed. Of all of them, surely the most incongruous must the *The Anglers Monthly* Rock and Pop Awards presented each year by Jack Charlton. The award for 'Best Song About a Fish' is won each year by Schumann for his song, 'The Trout', but in the tradition of such events, he has never been available to receive the award in per-son. The prize for 'Best Song About Fresh Water Trout Farming' remains unwon for the sixth year running – since its introduc-tion, in fact – and the 'Most Promising Newcomer to the Music Scene Whose Debut Single Mentions Salmon At Least Twice' award was a close run thing this year, but in the end, no-one won that either.

---

*As well as the BPI there are of course the BARMI awards – the Barnsley Awards to the Record and Music Industry – where the sinners receive a coveted BARMI – a little statue of a man sticking his tongue out with his trousers round his ankles. No-one won the either.

HOW TO BE A
ROCK
STAR

A guide to how to score in the rock world – apart from finding yourself a reliable drug dealer.

*DO NOT TRY TO PULL THIS SECTION OUT

DOING THE BUSINESS

Agents, pluggers, P.R. men, promoters, publishers, managers, publishing promoters, promotion managers, managing publishers, managing promotion publishing promoters, and cleaners. How does the record industry work? In fact, how on earth does it work with such dingbats in charge? What follows is an in-depth no-punches-pulled exposé of the 'Land of the Little Light Lunch (from midday to half-past-four)'. The only business to keep shorter hours than the banks.

PLUS a look at those on the fringes of the rock world – the hangers-on, liggers, free-loaders, groupies and other record company employees.

And the record company themselves: are they tightly-run, highly cost-conscious and efficiently managed businesses? Or are they hopelessly inefficient, ramshackle gin palaces stocked with shambling amateurs who are permanently out to lunch?

We asked one of the major recording companies to put their side of the argument. But unfortunately, they were out to lunch. So we joined them, and after a couple of stiff cognacs and a bottle of '76 Chateau La Fitte, we came to the conclusion they are tightly-run, highly cost-conscious and efficiently managed businesses.

HOW DOES IT ALL START?

Every year thousands of young hopefuls trudge through the doors of the major record companies, hoping for a break. So what are the talent scouts looking for? Dawn Grigson has been Head of A&R at Trick Records for 5 years now, and she still doesn't know what A&R stands for. She 'belled' us when she had a 'window in her Filofax' and allowed us to talk to her for 3½ minutes she told us:

'My first question with any artist is this: 'do they have legs?'* If they do, then I feel we can get into bed together.† But obviously only if they have the talent. And when we're talking talent, we're talking looks. We're talking great make-up, great clothes and a great bum.‡ Something that jiggles nicely in a video. And as for the girls, they need all that plus a great pair of tits. Of course, there's no need for them to sing – we've got little black boxes that can do that. Press a few buttons and you can make Andrew Ridgeley sound like Pavarotti. But they do need to be able to crash racing cars, and ponce around in the video. In fact the video's the most crucial thing of all. You have to have someone who looks sexy in a video, to make sure you sell the records, to pay for the bloody expensive video.'

WHAT HAPPENS THEN?

The next step for a band is to sign the contract. But beware the small print, as Rolo McGuigan, lead singer of Sprunt recalls:

'We were very green when we signed our first contract. We didn't check out the small print, so we didn't notice that it entitled our manager not only to 50% of our income, but also 50% of our houses and a 25% share in our girlfriends. Plus the right to use our toilet facilities 24 hours a day. In addition, in the slightly smaller print, there was a clause which said that we were not allowed to record for anyone else before we died. Well, all the wrangles got too much for our lead guitarist, Dave, who topped himself. Unfortunately he'd failed to read the small print that was written in micro dots where it said he was still contractually bound to go on performing regardless of being dead. In the end, our manager liquidated us and sequestered our assets. But he still comes round and uses the toilet all hours of the day and night.'

WHAT HAPPENS AFTER THAT EXACTLY?

Once a deal is signed and sealed, a band goes into the recording studios to lay down a few tracks and after they've injected themselves with heroin, they record some songs. Some attempt to push back the musical barriers and outdo their contemporaries. And some aim even higher and attempt a third chord. But most settle for leaving the difficult work to session musicians. Certain groups, leave everything to session musicians, including sleeping with groupies and taking drugs.

THEN WHAT?

The album complete, there then follows the problem of making the public sit up and take notice. This is where the marketing and promotion departments of the record companies come into their own. Janice Diller, Virgin*:

'We've got to always come up with new things, new concepts, to break through.

---

*do they have legs? – are they liable to succeed?
†get into bed together – negotiate a working contract.
‡a great bum – a great bum.
*Janice Diller works for W.E.A. Records.

Head of A&R at Rancid Records in conference with his accountant.

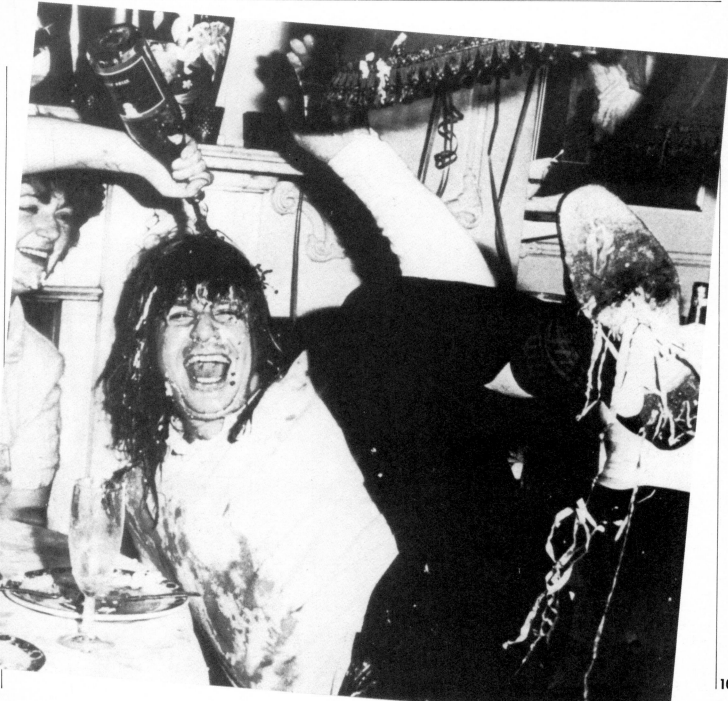

There's the "give-away" syndrome, for example, where you give away pens, posters, t-shirts and so on. In fact last year I had the brilliant idea of giving away the record. Giving away the record to make people go out and buy it.

'Then someone pointed out that they wouldn't buy the record if you'd just given it to them free, so we had to scrap that one, unfortunately. So we turned out attention to advertising gimmicks. We were the first to advertise albums on bus shelters for example. Then we did the same on milk bottles, but the bravest so far has been the adverts we printed on toilet rolls. Quite a novelty, really, wiping your bum on Nana Maskouri.'

HOW MUCH CORRUPTION IS THERE WHEN IT COMES TO GETTING RECORDS INTO THE CHARTS, THESE DAYS, I WONDER, WHAT WITH HYPING AND EVERYTHING?

Of course the music business has long been beset by rumours of illegal inducements to play records. Money, holidays, even sex has been offered. But the reverse is also true. In 1987, for example, 'The Irish Rover' was hyped into the charts by members of the Pogues and the Dubliners offering *not* to have sex with any disc-jockeys.

Corruption, graft, bribery, palm-greasing, lures, pourboires, dash and baksheesh … These are just some of the terms you will not hear used in the music business. Dr. Fitzgerald's recently published and

Left *The Pogues.*
Right *Allan Klein demonstrates his system of double barrelled book keeping.*

even more recently remaindered book on the subject, includes a glossary of terms that you *will* hear in the corridors of the modern record company:

> **GLOSSARY OF TERMS**
> *Creative marketing* ....Corruption
> *Creative accounting* ......Tax Evasion
> *Creative identity promotional expenditure* ....Hype
> *Positive positional chart adjustments* ....Chart-rigging
> *Ensured broadcast investment* ..Payola
> *Fiscal benefit inducement* .....Bribery
> *Reverse manual donations* ......
> Back- handers
> *Enforced surgical genuflection* ..
> Knee- capping

BUT HOW EASY IS IT TO GET INTO THE CHARTS IF YOU'RE NOT AN ALREADY WEALTHY AND ESTABLISHED BAND, THEN?

A good question. And one which Dawn Grigson shed some light on:
'It's not difficult at all. All new bands need to do is get on *Top of the Pops*. Unfortunately, of course, you can't get on *Top of the Pops* unless you're in the charts. But, you know, you can get into the top 50 just on the strength of a good video. And most companies spend a hell of a lot on videos for new bands. Any new band that gets into the top 50 in fact. Some people say it's a bit of a Catch 22 situation, but I don't think you can really say that until you've proved that it is. And of course, in order to prove that it is, you have to say that. So there it is.'

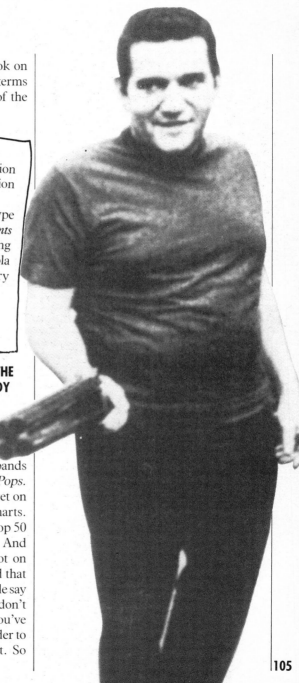

THE MEDIACRITIES OF LIFE

THE WORLD OF 'POP MEDIA' – POP VIDEOS, POP MAGAZINES, POP TV SHOWS, ROCKUMENTARIES, ROCK OPERA, ROCK MOVIES, ROCK HUDSON.

AND WE ASK ...

'Did video kill the radio star? And if so, was it justifiable homicide?'

'How do people who couldn't find their way around the Central line, get to host *The Tube*?'

'Do you have to be highly qualified to work on the rock papers? Or can any illiterate, beer-guzzling bigot do the job?'

'And why is it writers of rock histories can't saem to spell the simplest word?'

VIDEO ... VIDEO ... VIDEO ... VIDEO ...

Has video killed the radio star? Radio itself has of course evolved enormously from the first primitive cats whiskers of the 1930s to the sophisticated digital cats whiskers of the 1980s. But video is certainly everywhere nowadays, mainly because it's crucial to a record's success. Consequently, top directors such as former pop stars-turned-art students, Cobbley & Green are much in demand. Here is what happens on a typical day's shoot. This was during their latest project for Trouser Experience.

THE MAKING OF A VIDEO

The video is a fantasy set in the decadent splendour of 18th century Versailles. And

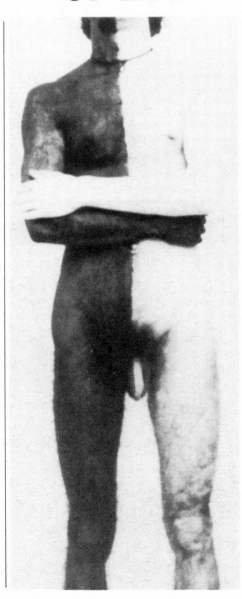

so Cobbley and Green have decided to shoot it in Coventry.

The opening shot they decide should be of the outside of a television studio in Coventry. So the set builders have been up all night making an exact replica of the one they're in. Eventually, Kevin Cobbley, the more bearded of the two, decides he doesn't like it, as it looks too authentic. He tells them to tear it down, and use the building they're in instead.

By lunchtime they have the opening two frames – that's one seventeenth of a second.

Over lunch the 1400 extras for the fantasy sequence arrive, in time to have their private parts painted purple.

At 2 o'clock shooting begins with the members of the band.

Martin Martin, lead vocalist, has done one shot of him being sad, and another being happy. Unfortunately they both look the same, so the hunt is on for a different facial expression.

By tea-time the next 7 frames – that's nine-seventeenths of a second – are 'in the can'. The directors are ecstatic, the band tired, and the extras, having hung around doing nothing for 4½ hours, have their private parts washed, and are asked to come back at the same time tomorrow.

Only seven months later, the final edited video is ready. The cost has come out at

An extra's part.

around £800,000, but the record company have insisted on paying double to ensure a higher chart position.

The video went on to win the much coveted V.D. Arts Award for 'Most Total Absence of Actual Group in a Video'. The directors also win awards for 'Best Use of Old Car in a Video' and the 'Phil Collins – Philip Bailey Award for Most Artificial Use of Group Pretending They Weren't Being Filmed'.

THE AGE OF VIDEO

There's no doubting we live in the Age of Video – a time when Art has fused with Rock to form 'Arck'.

'Thriller' stands as the biggest-selling album of all time, and also the biggest-selling video of all time. Michael Jackson managed to spin it out to 15 minutes by copying some elaborate special effects that he'd seen in the film *American Werewolf in London*. John Landis was the director of both that film and the video. So how did he feel when he was asked by Michael Jackson?

'It was like Christmas! I mean, I'm sitting there minding my own business and along comes this four-year-old kid with a lot of money and asks me to do something I've already done. I tell you, if that's rock & roll, I love it!'

The video entitled *The Making of Thriller* became the second top-selling video of all time, and will probably only ever be outsold by the planned sequel, *The Making of the Making of Thriller*. It has been estimated that every household in Britain owns either the 'Thriller' album, or a hit single from it, or owns the video of it, or has seen the video of the video.

Michael Jackson after his latest plastic surgery.

However, after months of research, the one person in the Western Hemisphere who had never heard any of 'Thriller' nor seen it on video, was traced. That person was Mrs. Ida Jenkins who lives on the Island of Sark in the English Channel. She is 98 years old, stone deaf, totally blind, and very, very happy.

RADIO ... RADIO ... RADIO ... RADIO ...

The most vital part of the Rock Media is radio. And the most vital part of radio are the disc-jockeys. And the most vital parts of disc-jockeys don't bear thinking about. But their importance cannot be over-looked, however much we might like to.

To a disc-jockey or 'jock' as they're known in the trade, image is all. As can be seen by the wide variety of styles around:

The Mike Read Look – sunglasses with satin bomber jacket advertising a rock tour of the nineteen-seventies.

The Simon Bates Look – a style made popular by John Travolta. The wide collar, open neck, etc, now only worn by middle-aged DJ's who have failed to cross over to television.

The Steve Wright Look – the main feature of this is the tie, which looks as if the wife has tied it for him as he went out the door and he's angrily undone it as soon as he's got around the corner.

The Anne Nightingale Look – also called the Shirley Williams Look, which is achieved by being carefully pulled through a hedge backwards every morning.

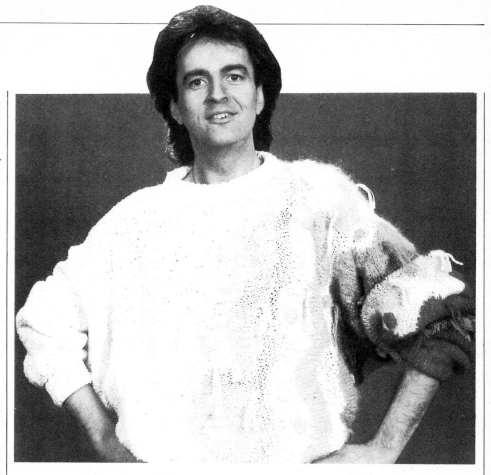

Above The DJ-Who-Has-Made-It-To-TV Look – the main feature here is the embarrassing sweater which always come from either *The Val Doonican Show* wardrobe, or else has been hand-knitted by a grateful, blind viewer.

The Andy Kershaw Look – the aim of this is to look so ordinary that you stand out in a crowd.

The Local Radio Look – the ill-fitting t-shirt that carefully exposes the navel, and the baggy jeans that fall elegantly to the floor when you go downstairs.

Deciding on a radio station's music policy calls for a good deal of delicate but firm judgement. Gerald David, former Head of Carpets at the BBC and now programme controller of Radio Bedrock, has the problem of programme planning down to a fine art:

'In the mornings it's strictly Top-40, some folk, a little new wave, a bit of jazz, blues and gospel, mainstream, off the wall stuff. Then in the afternoons, we aim at house-wives, men at home, men at work, school-children, and retired people down the library. So it's very much the mums and dads, heavy metal, electro funk, Vera

Lynn, Billy Bragg, Chaka Khan mix that we look for. And then in the evenings, it's hip-hop, top 10, atonal electronics, with Reginald Dixon at the Blackpool organ. All in all, I suppose our output tends to be middle of the road, Paul Young style, freaky independent punk specifically right across the board sort of stuff.'

MOVIES … MOVIES … MOVIES … MOVIE

Ever since Elvis Presley made his first film in 1956, and remade it 138 times over the next ten years, rock stars have been lured by Hollywood. But the film industry has shown very little originality in its treatment of rock, relying mainly on remaking old movies. Thus Barbra Streisand was in the fourth re-make of *A Star Is Born*, which was later remade by Sting as *A Star Is Bored*, and is to be remade yet again with Morrissey as *A Bore Is Starred*.

Today more and more rock stars are appearing in films. Bob Geldof starred in *The Wall* and was amazingly convincing in the title role. However his next film *Number One* was so bad that it had to be heavily edited before it was considered good enough to be thrown away.

The most essential ingredient for a successful film now is a hit song, with the record plugging the film, the film plugging the record, and so on, in a never-ending cycle. Graham Kent of 'Too Many Cooks Spoil The Broth' has first-hand experience of this:

'We wrote this song for a film which everyone really went for, but unfortunately the film turned out to be a real turkey. So they decided to scrap the film and make another one, based on our song. But then they needed a new song to go with it, and the new song we did wasn't as good as the old song, so the film didn't take off. So they got someone else to do a song for it, but by that time the film had flopped. The thing was they really liked these other guys' song, so they asked us to write a film around it, and that's what we're doing. You never know, there might be a record in it.'

MUSIC PRESS … MUSIC PRESS … MUSIC P

Statistics show that of all people who buy music papers, 64% buy them to use as toilet paper, 32% to put down on the kitchen floor after it's been washed, and the remaining 4% to read – as an alternative to sleeping pills. Why should this be? A look at a typical page in the new teen smash mag *Number 2's* shows some of the reasons for its decline in popularity.

It was during the court case following the publication of the above quiz, that it emerged that the answers were to the previous week's questions. (Not that that stopped Ms. Easton's lawyers suing for every penny they could get.)

But the lawsuits don't seem to deter the hardened rock columnist. Leslie Anne Blake, for example, once described Madonna as 'The greatest talent in the history of the known universe', and a week later as, 'the biggest bore in the history of the world'. This was, she claimed, because Madonna needed taking down a peg or two as the was starting to think she was the greatest talent in the history of the known universe.

Leslie's column in *The Daily Nipple* has done much to boost the newspaper's circulation, but at what price?

ACROSS:
1. Ben E. King's middle n

DOWN:
1. D.I.V.O.R.C.—. sang
nette (1).

POP QUIZ

Shag, with Jonathan King.

While the re
have gone i
funk-rock,
Andy Taylor
the answer
heavy meta
glossy prod
isn't so mu
lump of old
inspiration
Taylor has
Steve Jone
songs. An
sing bette
Le Bon, b
songs are
tonsils m
Life Goes
scarf-wa
Thunder
though *B*
be a gian
Adam S

★★

Much th
has gon
album.
hit, *Th*
Money
More
Hollyw
been a
instru
result
and in
Nicole

★★

QUESTIONS
1. What was Paul Young's first solo hit?
2. When did Phil Collins become lead singer of Genesis?
3. How many children has Sting had?
4. Whom is Olivia Newton-John alleged to have married?
5. What did Sheena Easton do to get her big break?

ANSWERS:
1. Chirpy Chirpy Cheep Cheep
2. Neither
3. 1 in 1979, 3 in 1980 and 47 in 1981.
4. A Yellow Submarine
5. Shag Jonathan King.

UP AND COMERS

A LOOK AHEAD TO THE BANDS OF THE FUTURE

There's so many people who've said to me they think we're the band for tomorrow,' says Rolo McGuigan, lead singer of Sprunt. 'I play them some of our music, and they say "yeah, look I'd really like to hear more of that tomorrow or some time – I'm a bit busy right now".'

Rolo feels that 1988 could be their year though, as he explains: 'I really feel 1988 could be our year.' The band feel they've been unlucky with their singles so far – none of the 38 they've released have entered the Top 40. Or the Top 75. Or the Top 200. In fact, as far as they know no-one has actually bought one of their records. But Sprunt, or S.P.R.U.N.T. as they're known for short are certainly not down-hearted.

But why do they call themselves S.P.R.U.N.T. for short, when it takes three times as long to say as Sprunt?

Below *Sprunt*

'Enigma' states Rolo, and turns to gaze out of the window.

Rolo's been pretentious for 7 years now. Ever since he went to Art school where he in fact met the other members of Sprunt. 'We used to play ANYWHERE – children's parties, local pubs, wedding receptions' – but they weren't a great success. 'I think we'd have gone down better, if we'd been booked to do them instead of just gate-crashing like we did.' But one day they were 'spotted', as they say in the business (the criminal business, that is) and they were done for trespassing. Rolo looks back on those days with a mixture of hatred and loathing. 'They were bloody awful. In fact I came very close to killing myself – and I know a lot of the rest of the band did too. That's how much they hated me.' But things started to look up for them all. 'Things started to look up for us all.' A music publisher happened to see one of their live gigs, and offered them a record contract. All Rolo had to do was to put his signature at the bottom, and every month he would receive 3 top-selling albums at the recommended price and the 'Record of the Month'. With astute cunning, and the sort of observation for which Rolo is as yet still unknown, he realised this was not the sort of record contract they wanted. That decision turned out to be the the right one … 'The next day Alison, our bassist, happened to be sleeping with this record producer, and right out of the blue, we got this recording deal.'

So, the future for Sprunt looks bright, but in the end, what do they really want out of it? Just money and fame? Churning out record after record all sounding the same? A shallow existence of fast cars and women? 'Yes' says Rolo, 'that'd do fine.'

TROUSER EXPERIENCE

'I remember my Dad never really approved of me playing in a group and wanting to be a musician. He used to say, "As long as I'm alive, no son of mine's gonna end up a hippie!" Martin Martin, lead singer of Trouser Experience chuckles to himself, 'So I killed him.' Martin's early

Right Two members of Trouser Experience

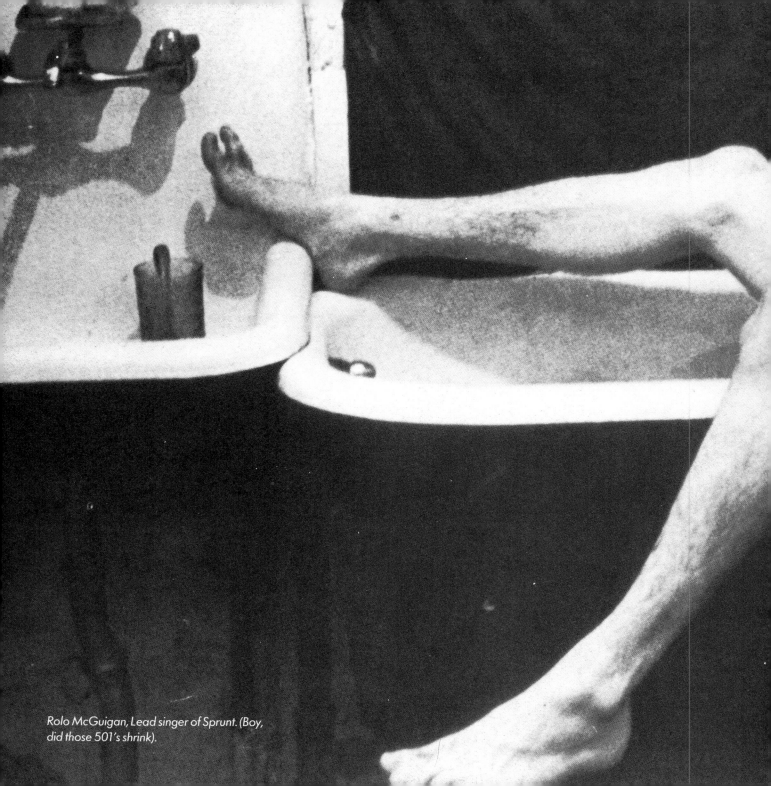

Rolo McGuigan, Lead singer of Sprunt. (Boy, did those 501's shrink).

days in Borstal have stood him in good stead though for the rigours of the music business. 'Now I know how to negotiate contracts for us. I just say, "'Ere, you know I shot my own father?" And they just seem to give us whatever we want.' Unlike so many other bands who met at Art School, such as 10CC and Sprunt, Trouser Experience first met up at Borstal.

Some of their early songs such as the classic 'I'm A Pink Banana With A Wife And Two Donkeys In Bagshot', show that the group not only have an unusual way with words, but severe psychiatric disorders. But that hasn't stopped them furthering their careers as pop stars. In fact, in many ways it's probably been an advantage. Deon McDermott is the main musical force behind the group and has some impressive credits to his name. He not only played spoons on John Lennon's 'Give Peace A Chance', but has appeared with Elton John at Wembley when a cameraman managed to catch him in the same frame, waving and shouting 'Hello, Mum'. Big-headed without being quietly confident, and musical without being talented, Deon agrees that there's a distinctive Irishness about their music, which he puts down to his ancestral influence and the fact all their music is played on bagpipes and a bodhran.

Their first LP, 'Inside Leg' was a big hit in Ireland, but some of the lyrics were considered too outrageous for an English audience. Songs such as 'I Hate Anyone Who's English', and 'Shoot All Those English Bastards And That Goes For Their Families Too', have not been kindly received by the British press.

'I don't deliberately set out to shock people,' says Deon spitting out the last piece of the live hamster he's been eating, 'I suppose it's just the way I am.'

But shocking or not, Trouser Experience are here to stay. As Deon puts it in one of his songs: 'We are the Duracells of life, let us light up the world – and keep charging!' Inspired Poet? Or mad Irishman? Whichever, there's no denying in the future the world will be gaining a lot more Trouser Experience.

THE BODY FLUIDS

Dean, Tonia, Ford and Jodie Freeman are all from a small surburban town in Louisiana. Not in itself remarkable, until you consider they are not in any way related. 'For some reason people are always asking us if we're brothers and sisters, just because we have the same name and come from the same street in the same town.' In fact, all four of them actually grew up in the same house, which makes it all the more unbelievable, especially when they eventually concede that they do share the same parents, but there's no denying they all have their own very different personalities.

Jodie, for example, has a sensational singing voice, whilst Ford is virtually tone-deaf. Strange, therefore, that Ford should be their lead-singer, with Jodie playing bass. Especially as Tonia has already been heralded as the Janis Joplin of her generation – destined to become promiscuous and die of a drug overdose at an early age.

But why 'The Body Fluids'?

'We went through a whole series of names,' explains Jodie, 'starting off with Vaseline and Liquid Penguin, on to Plastic Fists and the Beatless, until we finally decided we wanted a name that said something about the plight of the Red Indians in central America. So we called the band, "Something Ought To Be Done About Those Red Indians In Central America". But it didn't seem to catch on. Then Dean came up with this Body Fluids, which seemed to go down real well. So we stuck to it.'

They have to-date released one album cleverly entitled 'Body Fluids', most of which was written by Jodie. Many of her songs have been covered in the past by famous artists, such as the raunchy 'You Bring Out The Women In Me' which appears on the latest Muppets album, 'I take a lot of care over writing my songs. I keep refining the tune until it's in its purest state, reworking the lyrics until they complement the melody perfectly and then I give it to Ford to murder.'

There's clearly some resentment within the group which may or may not come from the fact that it's taken 5 years of working the club circuit to get this far. 'Playing clubs and discotheques was hard work. You'd really have to holler and scream to make yourself heard,' says Ford, 'although things got easier when they agreed to turn the disco off during our act.'

All that training has done them no harm at all though. They now have a world tour lined up with Anita Baker to Australia and the Far East, after which they hope to get back to work. But you can bet that whatever that work is, The Eighties will be the decade in which it's done.

Right *The Body Fluids.*

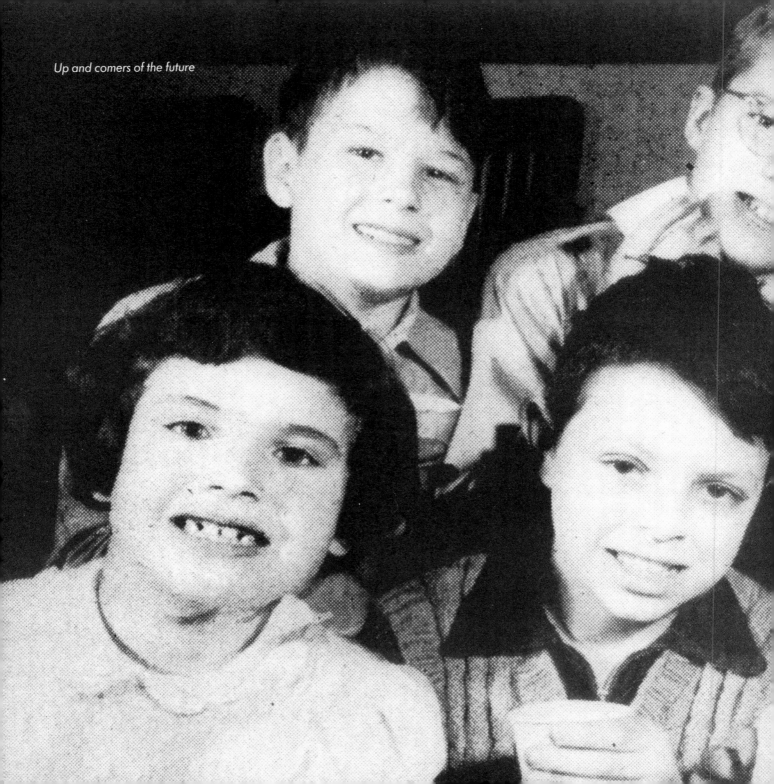

Up and comers of the future

EIGHT WAYS TO HAVE A HIT

HOW TO HAVE A HIT

1. One sure-fire way to have a hit in this day and age is to be married to Andrew Lloyd Webber. It should guarantee at least one hit a year, but what a hideous price to pay for chart success.

2. A less painful way to have a hit, is to simply give yourself an extremely silly name, such as Prefab Sprout, Fine Young Cannibals, or silliest of all, Harold Faltermeyer.

3. Another way to have a hit is to either appear on *Miami Vice* or write the theme music to it, as Jan Hammer did – a man who took his name from a Dutch firm of demolition contractors.

4. One extremely cheap way to have a hit is to appear on the TV rock show which is presented by a computer-projected version automaton who introduces the latest videos and is forever malfunctioning in amusing and ludicrous ways. And as well as *The Roxy,* there's *The Max Headroom Show.*

5. An absolute 100% certain way of having a hit is to have already had a hit in the late 1950s. A simple deal tying it in with a TV commercial for denim jeans will ensure an extended run at No. 1. And if you're a model with no singing or acting ability it helps to remove your trousers in a jeans commercial.

5A. If you're a woman with a bra size bigger than your I.Q. you can take your clothes off, pose for Page 3. Even if you don't have hits of your own, like Sam Fox, you'll be invited to take part in charity records where you'll be seen with 150 other nonentities, ruining the words in the video.

6. Around Christmas it is possible to have a hit by simply thinking of the worst song you can remember your grandmother humming, and recording it with the aid of bag-pipes or Roger Whittaker.

7. Finally, the most foolproof way of ensuring a No. 1 hit, is to release a single which sells more copies than anyone else.

Right *A typical roadie buying the weekend joint.*

PREDICTIONS FOR THE FUTURE

Michael Jackson, having failed in his bid to buy the remains of The Elephant Man from London Hospital Medical School, the doctors invited him to visit The Pathology Department because they want to examine a living prat.

Rock stars continue their campaign for Safe Sex. Duran Duran become Durex Durex (or Frankie re-record 'Relax' as 'Durex'), Madonna records 'Stay A Virgin' and Nancy Reagan jumps on the bandwagon by recording 'Da Do Ron Ron' as 'Da Don't, Ron, Ron!'

Simon Le Bon splits from Duran and then splits from himself to become Simon and Le Bon.

Russia stage a massive pop festival designed to demonstrate to the world that they are not as behind the times as everyone thinks. The concert is headlined by Freddie & the Dreamers and Rosemary Clooney.

Richard Branson sets off round the world in his yacht. Unfortunately, he accidentally makes it. The following month he sets out on the big one – to circumnavigate Alison Moyet. Richard Branson then sets off around the world in his hot air balloon. It ends in disaster when it crashes into the sea because he momentarily stops talking.

Dire Straits make a record with Chris Rea. The group is known as Chris Straits.

An ad hoc group of musicians including Cliff Richard, Andy Summers and the Wombles come together to make a record in aid of impoverished citrus fruit farmers. They call themselves Lemon Aid.

Pepsi & Shirley update their image for the 1990's by changing their name to Diet Pepsi & Shirley.

Julian Lennon shocks religious Americans by announcing that he is more famous than his father. Devout believers in John burn his son's records in protest.

The trend for groups to get together to record continues. Human League and Prefab Sprout combine to form Human Sprout, Men Without Hats and The Dooleys become Men Without Dooley's, and Meatloaf, Fish, and Blancmange combine and the result is Indigestion.

Status Quo play their final final gig. It is held at the Natural History Museum after which they are stuffed and mounted. They find it extremely pleasurable.

Her Majesty the Queen tops the charts with a rap version of her Christmas message.

Genesis become the biggest ever album-selling band in the history of rock, and as a mark of their standing in the business, an adjective is coined to describe their music, "Genesidal".

Annie Lennox splits from David A. Stewart, and re-releases an old Eurythmics track as tribute to him. It is entitled 'Thorn In My Side'.

Sir Bob Geldof becomes Lord Geldof for his services to music and the community in not releasing any more records.

Devout Christian, Alvin Stardust retires from the music scene in order to become closer to Goddard.

1999 – A new fashion emerges, the ultimate in nostalgia: leopard skins, tooth necklaces, bare feet and long straggly hair. They live in caves, eat raw meat, say only the word 'ug', and listen to Radio One.

The Housemartins win a BPI Award for being the first group of city stockbrokers sons living in the home counties to become a working class group of Northerners from Hull.

Samantha Fox has another hit with a record called "Oooh Touch Me, Lick Me, Rub Me In Butter, But Just Remember I Want To Be Treated As A Serious Singer And Not Just A Page Three Girl".

Adam Horowitz of the Beastie Boys is arrested and charged with being in possession of a silly name. He agrees to change it to John Horowitz.

A new male singer breaks with tradition by becoming successful without ever being sexually linked to Paula Yates.

The Beastie Boys, who claim to be influenced by Young Ones star, Ade Edmondson, continue to follow his lead and indulge in the ultimate anarchy: they start to do commercials for the National Westminster Bank.

Alison Moyet puts on another stone and becomes a genuine all-round entertainer.

Starship, formally the acid group Jefferson Airplane, continue to have hits with the sort of records that conclusively prove that drug-taking in the 60's *DID* destroy the brain cells.

The-The merge with Talk-Talk to form The Talk - The Talk. ABC combine with AC/DC and A-ha to become Abcacdcaha.

George Michael is rejoined by Andrew Ridgeley. Nobody notices for six months.

The Smiths announce that, following their 'Meat Is Murder' campaign, they will not be performing any more live concerts in front of their fans, as they can no longer condone cruelty to vegetables.

INDEX

HOLDER, LOO ROLL (See uses for at after concert parties 90)

IFIELD, FRANK (Big down under, or is that just a bit of gossip? 39)

JACKSON 5 (STONEWALL JACKSON, JERMAINE JACKSON, NOT PARTICULARLY JERMAINE TO THE ISSUE JACKSON, ABSOLUTELY NOTHING TO DO WITH IT JACKSON, JACKSON NICHOLSONSON & POLLOCK (JACKSON) 73)

JAN HAMMER (Dutch demolition contractor…see also theme to Miami Vice 67)

KERSHAW, NIK (See NIK KERSHAW'S RIDDLE ie Why was he so popular? 62)

KING (See B. B., BEN E., PAUL (See also HENRY VIII) (for which see Joe Brown and the Bruvvers) (see me poor spelling)

LIZZIE, THIN (Mad exercise woman on TV A.M. 89)

McTELL, RALPH (5)

McTELL, WILLIAM (Scottish hero who shot a pint of heavy off the top of his son's head with a crossbow 37)

McTELL, KISS AND (Legendary Scottish groupie 112)

MADNESS (See Kate Bush 67)

MADONNA (See under her Penn name 68)

MATLOCK, GLEN (54 See MALCOLM McLAREN and his contract with the SEX PISTOLS…hung by the matlocks)

MAY, BRIAN (See also DOBSON, ANITA

…just good friends)

MEATLOAF (32 1lb pork sausagemeat, 2 onions, 2 eggs, a slice of bread and 1 clove garlic (optional) 63) (That's waist size not page number)

MEN AT WORK (See Men no longer getting quite as much work as they were a few years ago 98)

MEL AND KIM (63 Unexpectedly popular singing duo comprising spy Kim Philby and comedian Mel Smith) (see Meatloaf)

MINDBENDERS (WAYNE FONTANA AND 90 also, MARIJUANA, L.S.D. and T.N.T. (see MIND EXPLODING) also see MIND EMPTYING…THE EUROVISION SONG CONTEST 63)

MICK (See DAVE DEE, DOZY, BEAKY AND TICH)

MOON, KEITH (origin of popular sports cliché…'Well Brian, I'm completely over the Keith)

NEW EDITION, NEW ORDER, NEW WAVE…HURRY! HURRY! HURRY! WHILE STOCKS LAST!!! (29)

NEWMAN, THUNDERCLAP (82)

NEWMAN, NANETTE (THUNDER-THIGHS) (48)

ONO, YOKO (64 as in O No, she's going to start singing again!)

PACEMAKERS, GERRY AND THE (78)

PACEMAKERS, HEART (See GARY GLITTER, BILL WYMAN etc)

PRINCE (see PURPLE, TONGUE & MARBLES (LOST) 34, also see his concerts (not that you'll be able to in Britain)

POP, IGGY (85)

POP, YUCKY (1 to 98)

ROBINSON (SMOKEY 32, TOM 71, LEMON BARLEY WATER 4)

ROTTEN, JOHNNY (34) (See also ROTTEN, AWFUL AND PRETENTIOUS i.e. EMERSON, LAKE AND PALMER)

SADE (Whips, leather, riotous parties of …92)

SADE, MARQUIS DE (Soporific jazz style singer 67)

SIMPLE MINDS (see PAUL McCARTNEY'S GIVE IRELAND BACK TO THE IRISH, CULTURE CLUB'S WAR IS STUPID, and anything by BLACK LACE)

SMITHS (Social commitment of 65, whatever happened to the blue bags of salt in packets of…90)

SPECIAL A.K.A. (87 see also SPECIAL BREW, CARLSBERG) (See MOTORHEAD) (in fact the only way to see MOTORHEAD)

SPRINGFIELD, DUSTY (83 see also brothers RICK and BUFFALO 98, see also CAT STEVENS, indirect connection with)

STEVENS, CAT (9 see the PET SHOP BOYS …IT'S A SIN, MATTHEW AND SIN etc)

STARR, EDWIN (86 see his son RINGO, his mother ATLANTIC and second cousins FIVE) (a poor imitation of the JACKSONS but an excellent new grade of lead free petrol…see NELSON MANDELA)

STEWART, ROD (Humbleness of, sexual abstinence of…no actual entry)

10CC (See Japanese motor- bikes 64)

THE RIGHTEOUS BROTHERS (86)

THE SLIGHTLY FLAWED BROTHERS (15)

THE DOWNRIGHT DISGUSTING, DEBAUCHED AND DIRTY HABIT BROTHERS (see THE NOLAN SISTERS)

TICH (See DAVE DEE, DOZY and you know the rest by now)

TIGHT FIT (See MEATLOAF'S Trousers)

TOWNSEND, PETER (Drug addiction of 67, anti drugs campaign of 67, liaison with Princess Margaret 78)

TYLER, BONNIE (See ROD STEWART & KIM CARNES…are they all the same person, and if not how come we never see them together? 31)

VAN (HALEN 65, MORRISON 41, RENTAL (Yellow Pages) 96)

VICIOUS, SID (Silly snake who sang with the Sex Pistols 87)

HISSING SID (Major rock figure who sang with Captain Beaky)

WILLIS, BRUCE (See actors who can't sing; also see singers who can't act (Sting) and singers who can't act or sing but insist on doing both (Toyah)

WILSON (leading sixties figure who lost his marbles…see BRIAN and HAROLD)

WOMACK AND WOMACK (See WOMACK AND WOMACK)

WOW WOW (noise made by people who are stoned 11)

BOW WOW WOW (noise made by dogs who are stoned, see MALCOLM McLAREN 47)

WINGS (What do you call a dog with? …Linda McCartney…see 'always end an index on a good old joke')

THE EXPERTS

The authors would like to express their thanks to the distinguished experts who helped them in the writing of this book. They are:

DR. QUENTIN FITZGERALD, Professor of Lyricology at St. Geldof's College, Oxford and Visiting Lecturer in Break Dancing at Exeter University. Author of 'The Girl With The Completely Blank Look In Her Eyes – The Semiology of the Lyrics of Kate Bush', (pp 240; available from The Exeter University Press at £25 and everywhere else at 99p).

CHARLIE RONSON, the leading American musicologist, Rock Correspondent to 'The National Geographic Magazine' and Professor of Comparative Creativity at the University of Life, Southern California. Author of 'Bruce Springsteen – The Man, The Music, The Headband', (pp24; out of print).

SAM 'FRIEND TO ALL THE STARS' CHUCK, the veteran Hollywood entrepreneur who set every star from Elvis Presley to Madonna on the road to success. Author of 'Presley & Me', 'The Beatles & Me', 'Michael Jackson & Me', 'Madonna & Me', 'Sam Chuck & Me' and 'Me, Me, Me & Me – The Life & Times of Sam Chuck'.

And thanks to BERNIE OBERDORFF for moral support, good vibes, tea, sympathy and sex.

BIBLIOGRAPHY

The following is a list of books used for reference in the writing of this work.

THE FIFTIES

'AWopBopaLooBopaLopBamBoom! – The Lyrics of Little Richard' – *Dr. Quentin Fitzgerald.*

'AWopBopaLooBopaLopBambi! – The Lyrics of Walt Disney' – *Dr. Gerald Fitzquentin.*

'AWopBopaLooBopaLopBamboo! – Rock & Roll in China' – *T.S. Eliot.*

'The Joy of Sex' – *Dr. Alex Comfort.*

'The Comfort of Sex' – *Dr. Alex Joy.*

'Elvis Was My Father' – *Sir Arthur Penhardy, O.B.E., PhD, C.D. (Brigadier, Rtd.)*

'The Elvis Presley Nobody Knew' – *Anon.*

'Are You Lonesome Tonight?' – The Elvis Who Loved Me' – *Verna Stringridge.*

'Are You Lonesome Tonight? Then Phone Mandy On 994-76942' – *Mandy Massage.*

'Oggly Boggly Diddle Mumph Cheesburger – Elvis Presley In His Own Words'

THE SIXTIES

'Gone But Not Forgotten – The Rock & Roll Casualties' – *Brett and Finola Whimsey.*

'Forgotten But Not Gone – The Bay City Rollers' – *Paul Barnett.*

'The Beatles – An Authorised Biography' – *Roger Teale.*

'The Beatles – An Unauthorised Biography' – *Roger Teale.*

'A Cellarful of Boys' – *Brian Epstein.*

'I Was The One Hundred And Thirtieth Beatle' – *Robert Runcie.*

'With The Beatles' – *Peter Norman.*

'It Was 50 Years Ago Today – A Premature History of 1967' – *Charlie Ronson.*

'The Kinks And Me' – *Cynthia Payne*

THE SEVENTIES

'Elton John' – *Harry Thomas.*

'John Elton' – *Thomas Harry.*

'The Care & Maintenance of Lawnmowers' – *Bob Dylan.*

'Children Of The Seventies – The Bay City Rollers Story' – *Chris Hall.*

'Children In Their Seventies' – The Rolling Stones Story' – *Mandy Smith.*

'The D.J. Book' – *Moss Bros.*

'D.I.S.C.O. – The Radio One Book Of Reggae' – *Gary Davies.*

THE EIGHTIES

'Boy George Knew My Brother' – *Jan Moss.*

'Born To Run – The Bruce Springsteen Story' – *Roger Scott.*

'Born To Stagger – The Andrew Ridgeley Story' – *Simon Scott.*

'Sex & Drugs & Drugs & Drugs' – *Boy George.*

'Hip Hop' – *Dr. Rodney Trower, MD.*

ALSO RECOMMENDED

'Looking Good The Geldof Way'

'The Encyclopaedia of Rock – 35 years of Rock 'n' Roll' – *Jeremy Pascall.*

'The Encyclopaedia of Rock – 35 Million Years of Geological Formation' – *Prof. Andre Schrepeski.*

'The Encyclopaedia of Rock – 35,000 Sticks of Seaside Candy' – *Mrs Betty Bottom.*

'The Encyclopaedia of Wok – 100 different ways to make a Chinese cooking implement' – *Fu Kin Kow.*

'Babylon Hollywood – An exposé of showbiz scandal in 1st century Judea' – *Kenneth Iscariot.*

'Rod Stewart – A complete biography' – *Geoff Brown.*

'Rod Stewart – A complete bastard' – *Britt Ekland.*

'Britt Ekland – A complete bastard' – *Rod Stewart.*

'A-Z of Rock 'n' Roll' – *John Blake.*

'A-Z of Halifax' – *Ordnance Survey.*

'The Life and Loves of a She-Devil' (a biography of Paula Yates) – *Geoff Brown.*

'Inside The Beatles' – *Peter Norman.*

'Round the Private Parts of The Beatles' – *Peter Norman.*

'Licking Every Orifice of The Beatles' – *Peter Norman.*

'Rock 'n' Roll Legends of the Past' – *Geoff Brown.*

'Rock 'n' Roll Legends of the Future' – *Doris Stokes.*

'Rock 'n' Roll Legends of the Fifteenth century' – *Prof. A. J. P. Taylor.*

'Music And God' – *Cliff Richard (autobiography).*

'Music And Goddard' – *Alvin Stardust (autobiography.*

'Observer Book of Stones' – *Observer Press.*

'Observer Book of Byrds' – *Observer Press.*

'Observer Book of Earth, Wind and Fire' – *Observer Press.*

'Rock Stars in their Underpants' – *Paula Yates.*

'Rock Stars in Other People's Underpants' – *Paula Yates.*

'Rock Stars in their Overcoats' – *Paula Yates (remaindered).*

NOT RECOMMENDED

'The Illustrated History of Rock Music' – *Jeremy Pascall.*

ILLUSTRATIONS